Defence Acquisition for the Twenty-first Century

Defence Acquisition for the Twenty-first Century

Editor & Author

Bernard Jenkin

Assistant Editors and Authors

Chris Donnelly

David McOwat

Contributors

John Louth

Alan Macklin

Chris Parry

Jonathan Shaw

Henry Strickland

Dan Ward

With a foreword by Robert Fox

CIVITAS

First Published July 2015

© Civitas 2015
55 Tufton Street
London SW1P 3QL

email: books@civitas.org.uk

ISBN 978-1-906837-70-9

Independence: Civitas: Institute for the Study of Civil Society is a registered educational charity (No. 1085494) and a company limited by guarantee (No. 04023541). Civitas is financed from a variety of private sources to avoid over-reliance on any single or small group of donors.

All publications are independently refereed. All the Institute's publications seek to further its objective of promoting the advancement of learning. The views expressed are those of the authors, not of the Institute, as is responsibility for data and content.

Designed and typeset by
lukejefford.com

Printed in Great Britain by
Berforts Group Ltd
Stevenage, SGI 2BH

Contents

Supporting Essays

Editor and Author

Bernard Jenkin MP was first elected to parliament in 1992. He has subsequently served as Shadow Defence Secretary, where he campaigned for more equipment and greater funding. Between 2006 and 2010, he sat on the House of Commons Defence Select Committee. Today he is a member of the executive of the 1922 Committee of backbench Conservative MPs and was chair of the Public Administration Select Committee 2010–2015. He is a regular commentator on defence, security and foreign affairs and a contributor to *Diplomat* magazine. He has twice addressed the annual IRIS (Institut de Relations Internationales et Stratégiques) Paris conference on missile defence and was a member of the Chatham House European Security and Defence Forum, a three-year project looking at the future of NATO and EU Defence. He has also addressed conferences at Royal United Services Institute. In 2007, he authored a paper for Conservative Way Forward entitled *Defence Policy for the UK: Matching Commitments with Resources.*

Assistant Editors and Authors

Chris Donnelly CMG TD helped to establish, and later headed, the British Army's Soviet Studies Research Centre at RMA Sandhurst. Between 1989-2003, as special advisor to four NATO Secretaries General, he was closely involved in the evolution of NATO and the reform of the newly emerging democracies in Central and Eastern Europe. From 2003–2010 he ran the Defence Academy's Advanced Research and Assessment Group. In 2010 he became Co-director of The Institute for Statecraft. He has written three books and many articles on questions of security, strategy and statecraft. He has held appointments as specialist advisor to three UK Defence Secretaries (both Labour and Conservative) and was a member of Prime Minister Thatcher's Soviet advisory team. He is also currently advisor to the Foreign Minister of Lithuania; serves as specialist advisor to the House of Commons Defence Committee; is a Security and Justice Senior Mentor in the UK's Stabilisation Unit; edits the British Army's official yearbook; is trustee of the London-based charities *Active Change Foundation* and *Forward Thinking*; and sits on the official team responsible for scrutinising the current reform of the UK's reserve forces for the Defence Secretary.

David M. McOwat's research began at Glasgow University in 1970 on aeroelastic propellers. He joined RAE Bedford in 1973, where he worked on aeroelasticity, systems and software engineering. He served in MoD MB from 1988-1996 as a scientific advisor to ACDS (Concepts), as AD (Science) Joint Systems, and as Customer for Systems and Human Sciences in the Corporate Research Programme. He initiated the UK Synthetic Environments programme. In 1996 he joined DERA as a technical consultant, moving to Dstl in 2001 to work on knowledge and information agency. He was Senior Research Fellow in the Advanced Research and Assessment Group at the Defence Academy from 2006 until 2010.

Contributors

Professor John Louth is Senior Research Fellow and Director for Defence, Industries and Society at the Royal United Services Institute for Defence and Security Studies. He served as an officer in the Royal Air Force for 16 years before working as a consultant and programme director extensively throughout the defence and energy sectors, employed in both the BMT Group and QinetiQ. His work has included the audit and governance of the UK strategic deterrent; the implementation of risk-based governance regimes into energy businesses; UK Ministry of Defence and industry partnering initiatives, especially within the air domain; and the development of chemical, biological and radiological protection and responses. He spent part of his career in the Middle East running separate national programmes to develop commercial and defence capabilities across a number of Gulf states. Dr Louth has also worked as a senior advisor to the European Defence Agency on the development of pan-European procurement policies and practices. He teaches at Roehampton University Business School in London and is also a specialist advisor to the House of Commons Defence Select Committee.

Major General Alan Macklin CBE is a programme and project management practitioner and Deputy Chair of the Association for Project Management, the UK professional body. After 34 years in the British army, of which 20 years were in the defence equipment acquisition business, he joined CH2M HILL, the global number 1 programme management company every year since 2004 (according to *Engineering News Record*) where he has been involved in the Olympic Park and Thames Tideway Tunnels programmes.

Rear Admiral Chris Parry CBE spent 36 years in the Royal Navy as an aviator and warfare officer. As well as sailing every sea, he experienced regular operational tours and combat operations in Northern Ireland, the Gulf and the Falklands and commanded the destroyer HMS Gloucester, the amphibious assault ship HMS Fearless, the UK's Amphibious Task Group and the Maritime Warfare Centre. He also had five joint appointments, including Director General Development, Concepts and Doctrine, with responsibility for future operational and developmental issues relating to all three services. Nowadays, he runs his own strategic forecasting company and is a regular broadcaster, commentator and author, most recently with the best-selling *Down South – a Falklands War Diary* (February 2012) and *Super Highway: Sea power in the twenty-first century* (May 2014).

Major General Jonathan Shaw CB CBE retired after 32 years in the British army, the last ten working in or for Whitehall. He was Director Special Forces and General Officer Commanding Multi-Nation Division (SE) in Basra in 2007 where he commanded 8,500 troops from six nations, charged with withdrawing from Basra. He was then Chief of Staff Land HQ 2008-9, making him a senior staff officer of 2,500-strong HQ, responsible for a £6bn budget. Today he is the Chairman of OPTIMA, a user-driven C-IED and search consultancy. He is the author of *Britain in a Perilous World; The SDSR we need*.

Henry Strickland is a management consultant with long experience of organisational transformation and turnaround. His particular focus is the rapid and cost-effective transformation of organisations employing large numbers of people in both the public and private sector. He is a Senior Associate Fellow of the Institute for Statecraft in London, where he specialises in institutional reform, as well as a director of a number of UK and overseas companies.

Lieutenant Colonel Dan Ward is the author of *F.I.R.E.: How Fast, Inexpensive, Restrained and Elegant Methods Ignite Innovation* (Harper Business, 2014). He served for more than 20 years as an acquisition officer in the US Air Force, where he specialised in leading high-speed, low-cost technology development programmes for all the military services and the intelligence community.

Dan holds three engineering degrees and received the Bronze Star Medal for his service in Afghanistan. He is a senior associate fellow at the Institute for Statecraft as well as a non-resident fellow at the New America Foundation. His writings have appeared in a wide range of publications, including the *Boston Globe, Fast Company, Forbes, Small Wars Journal, Armed Forces Journal,* and the Pakistani Army's magazine Halal. He is also the author of *The Simplicity Cycle: A Field Guide to Making Things Better Without Making Them Worse,* published this year.

Acknowledgements

This paper and collection of essays could not have been produced without a considerable team effort. I am extremely grateful to all the contributors and to others who attended an initial seminar we organised back in 2012.

This was inspired by opposition to the merger of BAE Systems with EADS, which provoked questioning about the continued dominance of defence prime contractors on an ever diminishing defence budget. I would like to thank Chris Donnelly, who has been inspiring in the rigour of his thinking and in his devotion to better defence policy, as well as Dave McOwat, who has been instrumental in delivering the final edit.

I also thank my office team in the House of Commons, particularly my researchers: Peter Cannon who laid much of the ground work; and Ashley Coates who helped to complete the project. Finally, thank you to David Green and Civitas for inviting me to undertake this work in the first place, and for being so patient with us.

Bernard Jenkin MP
House of Commons
February 2015

List of Acronyms

BERD	Business Enterprise Research and Development
BIS	Department for Business, Innovation and Skills
CDM	Chief of Defence Materiel
CDS	Chief of the Defence Staff
CENTCOM	United States Central Command
CSR	Comprehensive Spending Review
DASA	Defence Analytical Services and Advice
DE&S	Defence Equipment & Support
DERA	Defence Evaluation & Research Agency
DESO	Defence Export Services Organisation
DoD	United States Department of Defense
Dstl	Defence Science and Technology Laboratories
EUCOM	United States European Command
FRES	Future Rapid Effects System
GOGO	Government Owned/Contractor Operated
MoD	Ministry of Defence
NAO	National Audit Office
NATO	North Atlantic Treaty Organisation

NSC	National Security Council
NSS	National Security Strategy
OCCAR	Organisation for Joint Armament Cooperation
PAAMs	Principal Anti Air Missile System
PACOM	United States Pacific Command
PDT	Pre-Deployment Training
PSC	Private Security Contractor
RAE	Royal Aircraft Establishment
RAF	Royal Air Force
RN	Royal Navy
SDSR	Strategic Defence and Security Review
SME	Small & Medium Sized Enterprises
SOCOM	United States Special Operations Command
TRANSCOM	United States Transportation Command
UAV	Unmanned Aerial Vehicle
UKTI	UK Trade and Investment
UNCLOS	The United Nations Convention on the Law of the Sea
UOR	Urgent Operational Requirement

Foreword

One of the main difficulties with British defence procurement is that it is conducted in a sea of diverse and competing timetables. Major defence industrial programmes take decades to mature. Political and media agendas and timetables are often creatures of the moment, governed by sudden fashion or an immediate demand in the electoral cycle.

Too often, the last people considered in the whole process are the end-users, the men and women of the armed services, the operators and fighters who bear ultimate responsibility for the defence of the nation and its interests.

One of the aims of this paper is to discuss how procurement of the right equipment can be given greater – and much needed – agility and flexibility. Serving men and women need to have the confidence that they are getting the equipment that most effectively suits the requirements of their jobs. Sadly, in my experience, this has not happened in recent campaigns. In this century, in Iraq and Afghanistan British soldiers have had to go on patrol in thinly protected 'snatch' Land Rovers, relics from service in Northern Ireland, which even there proved barely adequate. In the field the Bowman radio and battlefield communications – a system that took a decade to get ready – has broken down when needed most.

Huge programmes like the Eurofighter Typhoon and the two fleet aircraft carriers, Queen Elizabeth and Prince of Wales, have taken a quarter of a century to evolve. The Typhoon was originally conceived in the Cold War, and at the time of writing is still not 'mature' in the ground attack variant – the role in which it is needed most. Equally, the two carriers are unlikely to operate in the 'deep strike' mode for which they were designed primarily.

In times of austerity and cutbacks, pursuit of the big programmes whilst economising in lesser ones has produced frustration among the operators and exposed critical gaps in capabilities. Among the casualties of the SDSR (Strategic Defence and Security Review) defence review cuts of 2010 was the over-budget and overdue Nimrod MRA4 maritime patrol aircraft. Unfortunately nothing was ordered to take on the role. The old Nimrod MR2s were taken out of service, and when not one, but two Russian nuclear patrol submarines sneaked towards the Scottish and Irish coasts in the summer of 2014, the UK had to call on patrol planes from France and America, having none itself.

Since 2010 there has been a heavy accent on balancing the books and shaping the ten-year big-ticket procurement programme, especially by Philip Hammond during his tenure as defence secretary. This has led to growing, and far from unfounded, fear that issues of personnel – in numbers, support and training – have taken second place. All three services have deficiencies in key areas, losing vital skill sets and capabilities. This has led the Royal Navy, for example, to offer contracts for marine engineering posts to US and Canadian navy and coastguard officers.

With further defence cuts in the wind for the CSR (Comprehensive Spending Review) and SDSR of 2015, further imbalances could be in prospect. If a disproportionate amount of the defence budget goes on equipment, there won't be the numbers of personnel in the ranks to man and maintain it all. New threats will require new skills and new categories of employment, and it will be expensive. The Army's new 77 Brigade has been formed for the new forms of asymmetric, information and cyber operations, and will require the recruiting and training of specialists, and this will be expensive.

The heirs of Tommy Atkins, the men and women in the forces today, have a vote in the future conduct of defence, security and foreign policy – which politicians and civil servants sometimes try to ignore.

Policy, or strategy, operations, personnel and management and the agile procurement proposed by this Civitas book, must be carefully coordinated in the defence and security architecture Britain requires today. They are complementary elements. Too often in recent experience the parts in this sum have operated separately. This is the conclusion of Christopher Elliott's examination of British military operations in Iraq and Afghanistan, *High Command*,[1] and Britain in a *Perilous World*,[2] an essay on strategy shortcomings by Jonathan Shaw, who writes later in this paper.

Both point to failures of internal communication in government and the military command. Here the context in which strategy and policy is set is vital. The context of both British campaigns in Iraq and Afghanistan changed so radically and so quickly that the whole policy and concept of operations should have been re-examined and analysed – the famous 'Question Four moment' in Army jargon – but never was.

The examination of context applies to defence and security planning and policy, including agile procurement, across the board. The perception of context is driven – especially in Britain – by the twists and handbrake turns of the media and political narrative.

Just look back a year, to January 2014, and who would have imagined the media narrative for the year would be dominated by fighting in Ukraine, the rise of ISIS / ISIL in Syria and Iraq, the halving of the price of oil and the Ebola pandemic? All have impacted defence, security and foreign policy. And in the first weeks of 2015 who would have predicted the dominance of the crisis in Greece and the jihadi attacks in Paris dominating the news media narrative?

The influence of the media narrative, the complex conversation through print, broadcast, internet and social websites, in policy making is underestimated – a point highlighted by Lord Peter Hennessy in his essay 'Establishment and Meritocracy'.[3] The UK government and advisory think tanks so far have produced nothing of the range, depth and foresight of the US National Intelligence Council's four-year horizon scans in the 'Global Trends' series.[4] Human geography is too often regarded as a Cinderella subject in British strategic studies. The understanding of humans in an increasingly complex social and physical terrain should be a necessary part of the policy maker's toolbox.

This applies in all aspect of defence and security, including acquisition and procurement.

Robert Fox
Defence Correspondent, *London Evening Standard*
February 2015

Overview

To fight and conquer in all your battles is not supreme excellence; supreme excellence consists in breaking the enemy's resistance without fighting.

Sun Tzu

A New Approach to Defence Acquisition

The main argument of this paper is that we need a completely new approach to defence acquisition. This is not to denigrate the MoD's recent efforts, nor to decry much of the thinking that has gone into defence acquisition in recent years. Nor is it to claim that all the thinking in this paper is 'new', but by bringing this together, we hope we can promote a deeper and more comprehensive understanding of the scale of the new thinking which it is imperative to apply.

The problem at the moment is that the message control hatches are battened down; debate about the real issues facing defence policy are being avoided at all costs. In fact, the money is not there to buy all the planes for the carriers that are presumed in the present policy.[1] Nor is there sufficient money to replace the Army's worn out kit or exhausted stores, let alone re-equip the Army through a new acquisition programme.[2] Iraq and Afghanistan have 'used up' most of the UK's land warfare capacity and, instead of planning to reconstitute this, it is being scaled back. The UK is providing the same number of combat aircraft as Belgium in the fight against ISIS. With the exception of the nuclear deterrent, which remains a 24-7-365 capability, the Royal Navy now is below critical mass; a strategic capability which is becoming sub-strategic in scale and military effect. Unlike the Royal Navy that sailed to the Falklands, it would be unable to sustain losses and still function. The ability to sustain losses in conflict is intrinsic to the ability to sustain military effect.

To talk about 'no strategic shrinkage' (as the Foreign Secretary did at the start of the last parliament) is incompatible with what we have done to the size and capability of the UK's diplomatic service and armed forces. We either have to spend more, or do things differently, or give up the idea of getting involved in any campaigns that rely on sustained diplomatic effort or military deterrence, let alone on the ability to deliver force. The politicians still behave as though the UK has the same power as ten or twenty years ago, but that is an illusion, which is positively dangerous.

Furthermore, the implication of the 2014 Autumn Statement is that defence may be cut yet further – none of the three main party leaders have said anything to the contrary. Indeed, earlier in 2015, the Prime Minister, David Cameron, did not deny it in his response to the BBC's Andrew Marr and his pointed questions in his New Year interview. Government and opposition have decided that 'there are no votes in defence'. The only way to contain the annual deficit is to cut in areas that are not perceived as election winners. If we (and other, particularly US, commentators) are misreading the Autumn Statement, then there is plenty of opportunity to let us know. For defence, it appears to be only about retrenchment; there are aspirations and high-minded objectives, but nothing to connect them with the actual defence capabilities we have. Nor is there much about how we are going to improve our defence economy; about how we will become more capable of competing as a power in tomorrow's world to preserve global, and our own, security; nothing to show that anyone at the top understands how important our acquisition system could be helping to revive our industry and economy.

Add to this the growing instability, especially in the Middle East where we are tied into supporting the US; the need to be able to fight with the new 'weapons' of 'ambiguous warfare' – economic, financial, cyber, information etc. – as well as with the classic kinetic ones; the issue of how we actually acquire the capabilities we need, and this becomes even more important than it was only a year ago.

Whatever happens, our acquisition system is no longer compatible with today's defence budget and so is in an impossible mess. The failed GOGO proposal succumbed to reality and to sustained criticism about how incompatible it was with 'agility' and control over defence policy, but the offer of our entire acquisition system to two foreign companies is subject to many of the same failings. The MoD risks losing even more competence, experience and expertise to its contractors, instead of building it up in-house so it can control its own programmes.

Defence acquisition is fundamental to our national security. It both underpins and reflects defence policy and forms a component of our strategic concepts. It is one of the main functions of MoD, but not its purpose. MoD exists to formulate and implement defence policy, which in turn supports national security and foreign policy objectives, which are drawn together and implemented as national strategy (i.e. 'grand strategy'). The uncertainty in the world demands that our security be provided by a community that is agile, adaptable and able to be restructured quickly as circumstances require. This includes our acquisition system. Introducing a contractual-based system hardly meets this need, nor does one based on five-yearly reviews.

Acquisition's place in this system is to contribute to advancing UK interests by providing the equipment and services needed both to deter and to counter threats and to create or exploit opportunities. It underpins our defence and deterrence postures. Through this, it has also generated and sustained much of our leading-edge industrial and commercial competitiveness.

Acquisition is distinct from purchasing, which is no more than buying equipment and services; and from procurement, where the buyer works with the supplier to deliver equipment or services to meet a need. While acquisition includes purchasing and procurement, it also involves the whole life-cycle of the capabilities and associated capacity we need. Consider acquisition as a 'strategic' activity, procurement as 'operational'.

Contrary to the public perception, MoD has continuously developed its acquisition organisation. This must have severely challenged the staff involved. It is not surprising that many have left, judging by the downsizing that has accompanied the changes. Defence Equipment and Support (DE&S) is on target to reach 10,000 by 2015 from a staff of some 22,300 in 2010. Nevertheless, those who have remained have successfully delivered equipment to support both the equipment programme and the many campaigns the UK has engaged in during this period, mainly using urgent operational requirements (UORs). This latter process has a much lower overhead than that used for the equipment programme and suits the much shorter timescales of campaigns. However, some thousands of (mainly small value) UORs have been raised and satisfactorily delivered, primarily by the SMEs. This must be recognised and all concerned deserve praise. This UOR process should become the dominant acquisition process from now on, rather than remaining as a secondary procurement process. Very expensive equipment may warrant other approaches. MoD must be free to employ whatever methods are appropriate, not forced to adopt a simplistic one-size-fits-all. However, the dramatic shrinkage in the size of Defence Equipment and Support (DE&S) will reduce our capacity to run UORs, result in a loss of competence in acquisition, and limit where we buy and how. This in turn will limit defence policy.

Working with a smaller defence budget

The reality we face is that, in drastically reducing our defence budget, we are similarly reducing our defence and industrial capabilities. The painful truth is that, on two per cent of GDP, we cannot maintain the kind of robust defence structure we did in the past, where we were able to organise and equip our armed forces; to match all potential competitors and to undertake all likely contingencies simultaneously; to support all our foreign policy objectives through influence and deterrence; and to cope with all the non-combat tasks they might be called upon to perform. It is dishonest to claim that we can rely on a technological advantage over competitors or potential adversaries. This is to ignore reality. The reductions in our research budget highlight the problem.[3]

We are unlikely to recover either our defence budget or our capabilities in the way that we have traditionally understood them. More money and more equipment acquired as it was in times past is not a realistic solution to expect. Furthermore, we have now reduced our industrial and military capabilities to such an extent that, even with increased resources, we may be unable to recover our former levels of capability and capacity quickly, if at all. However, BIS is aware of the problem, and has launched a number of initiatives with industry to reverse the damage. Notable is the Aerospace Growth Partnership which has announced a £300m programme (so far) to begin regeneration of a UK Aerospace capability.[4] It is unclear what contribution MoD is making to this investment.

The next strategic defence and security review (SDSR), scheduled this year, is likely to involve further cuts and force reductions, rather than to address the key question as to what volume of investment in security will generate the highest overall value to the UK. On the current trajectory, like its 2010 predecessor, the next SDSR is likely to be another savings package rather than a genuine strategic review that generates value for the UK. If the nation is going to invest only two per cent of GDP in defence (and we have yet to hear a political party commit even to the NATO minimum of two per cent[5]), then it is all the more essential to ensure that that investment is relevant and delivers maximum value, balanced between deterring or combating threats and enabling the UK to exploit and create opportunities in peaceful relations with, and having influence over, other nations.

Defence best value for the UK

There is still a tendency in Whitehall to think of defence only in terms of kinetic force. But all across the world – if only we will look with open eyes – we are seeing that conflicts are now being waged with a wide variety of forms of power, of which the 'kinetic' is only one. We must in future be able to acquire, i.e. to generate and maintain, many more forms of power than we currently recognise, and to employ them in conjunction with classic kinetic power when the need arises. To this purpose, the development of 'defence reviews' to 'defence and security review' is a step forward, at least in aspiration.

There is a further issue to consider. Although the defence equipment budget in recent years has been only a small percentage of GDP, and today amounts to less than one per cent of GDP, this investment has had a disproportionate impact because it has stimulated the science and engineering base used by civil industry and academic research fields. Today, we have lost sight of this issue and, now that we have also allowed our science and engineering base to decline, this will have very adverse consequences. Our defence exports have historically formed a high proportion of our balance of trade, but will also decline unless this failure to invest is reversed.[6]

If we want better defence in future, and wish to sustain the UK's science and technology base and our defence exports, we need to think differently - not just about defence acquisition, but about how we approach defence policy as a whole. We need to focus on our research, educational, commercial and industrial capability: on how as a nation we can use these capabilities to generate the necessary forms of power when we need them. Only this approach will ensure that what the UK invests in defence and security generates the best overall value to the UK.

The problem with our present equipment programme

The present model of defence[7] policy is based on an attempt to assess future threats and to forecast what we might need our armed forces to do. These are the 'defence planning assumptions'. The defence budget is unrelated to these threats, or to the investment plans of our allies. The MoD signs contracts for the equipment programmes which it hopes will enable the armed forces to do those specific things, assuming our predictions turn out to be correct and that we can counter numerical superiority in the threats through the superiority of our equipment and people. The (essentially fixed) investment rate is unrelated to the budget needed to acquire these forces within meaningful timescales or to maximise the value of the investment.

This is often likened to an 'insurance policy', where we invest in defence equipment as an insurance against what we suppose we can predict might happen. This is the wrong model for the early twenty-first century. It is classic Cold War thinking which can only be effective when assessing known threats and known enemy capabilities. Since the end of the Cold War, this model of thinking has been disproved again and again. Even during the Cold War, the outset of the Falklands Campaign demonstrated the dangers of allowing this thinking to dominate. Instead, we should look at defence and security as an investment opportunity that contributes to advancing our interests constantly, not spasmodically or as a last resort. We cannot afford to invest in forces that are inappropriate to the campaigns we may have to wage.

The challenge we face with defence acquisition and our legacy equipment programmes is that they are subject to a level of cost inflation that is far higher than the general rate of inflation.[8] It may seem paradoxical, but this defence cost inflation is driven by competition between the major defence conglomerates as much as it is by peer-threats. Defence manufacturers design weapons to be the best in the world. Our defence equipment is designed not just to match and be better than that of our enemies, but to match or be better than the equipment of our allies too. The defence companies are constantly seeking to add capability and sophistication to their products and programmes, which we and our allies feel we must have in order to maintain our technological superiority and interoperability. This means that costs always escalate, while the number of units we can deploy always declines as the sophistication of the equipment increases. This is despite the fact that the adversaries our armed forces face today are for the most part far behind in technical sophistication or capability: they seek to derive their advantage in other ways.[9]

Hyper-competition can drive an industry to self-destruction and, unfortunately, defence is a prime example of this. The reduction in the Defence Budget to two per cent or less of GDP means that, henceforth, products will best be acquired by small-scale manufacturing techniques suited to the small inventories and, in general, based on civil rather than defence-specific engineering. This practice allows research to be fed directly into prototypes. This is important because, when we build such small numbers of major equipment, they are all, in effect, prototypes. In turn, this supports an agile equipment industry, better suited to compete in the world.

The problem with our present defence equipment programme is that it has now overtaken defence policy. The MoD is treated more and more as a means of delivering defence procurement contracts and a prescribed list of defence capabilities. The 2010 defence review (SDSR) was the first to be decided from outside the MoD; the National Security Council (NSC) took the final decisions and tasked the MoD to deliver the prescribed outputs. The vast majority of our projected future defence expenditure up to 2020 is tied up in existing projects,[10] as the then Defence Secretary Phillip Hammond made clear in his address to the House of Commons in May 2012.

This is not what today's defence needs. Everyone now agrees that we need an agile and flexible military capability, but this cannot be delivered by depending first and foremost on large and expensive equipment. Today's defence depends upon a strong and agile knowledge and expertise base, which is able to respond in times of crisis and at times when the UK's national interest requires it. A state spending only two per cent of its GDP on defence cannot have the 'robust' defence structure of previous decades. It must build a force for every campaign in a different way appropriate to that campaign. Moreover, that state – in this case, the UK – must avoid getting into campaigns it cannot build for. We have found in recent decades that the big defence programmes are no guarantee of success in theatre.

The new thinking: agile capability development

We therefore need to give the concept of 'agile capability' real meaning. Our priority target should not be capabilities *per se* but the capacity to generate the capabilities we need when we need them: equipment which is effective and cost-effective. This is not always to seek world-beating or state-of-the-art equipment. This means that we need to have the industrial capacity, the technical capacity and the intellectual capacity to do this. This capacity is required not only in the armed forces and the MoD, but also outside, in industry, commerce and the research base, and universities. More importantly, parliament and the political community must also have the intellectual capacity needed to lead the provision of our security. Since few will have direct experience to teach them, other means to provide this understanding are required.

Moving to an adaptable force structure in the coming years necessitates a revolution in our thinking and approach to defence acquisition. Unfortunately, there is little real understanding of this as a practical reality in parliament, government, our defence establishment or our industry. The key shift which we must make if we are to generate agile capability is to determine how, and how much, to divert defence spending to support agile funding for the security needs of the country on timescales which match the relevant business, development and research cycles. This cannot be on an annual basis. The MoD must be enabled to spend money when it needs to do so and to save it when it can, with the reassurance that the money saved will be available when needed.

Currently, MoD is subject to an inappropriate financing system, which encourages the buying of equipment at all costs to avoid 'underspend'; so people convince themselves that the equipment is essential. Emergency acquisition is funded by Treasury subventions through a process known as Urgent Operational Requirements (UORs). UORs are a form of defence acquisition process which proves the potential efficiency and effectiveness of a more agile approach. However, the present combination of the major programmes supplemented by emergency UORs creates possibly the most inefficient and clumsy way imaginable of mounting and supporting campaigns. It should be recognised that the UORs are an example of campaign-based acquisition, and that this should be formalised within MoD organisationally and managerially as the basis for agile acquisition.

Research and development

If we cannot design or synthesise equipment, we cannot make it. Research and development (R&D), is the crucial factor here. Throughout history, no military force that has sought to develop its own weapons has been able to do so without a vibrant and sustained research programme. Methods have changed, but the necessity for research, experimentation and prototyping has not.

Our spending on research has fallen to a fraction of what it was,[11] and narrowed as a consequence. The present defence industry in the UK is still living off the defence R&D investment made during the Cold War. Established best practice indicates that, across a portfolio of technical acquisition programmes, some 10 per cent of the cost should be allocated to research and 35 per cent to development in order to contain the system technical risks and ensure delivery timescales. The smaller the budget and hence production run, the larger the percentage which should be allocated to R&D to ensure the minimum of problems with the equipment. Clearly, smaller budgets will mean fewer developed systems with performance advantages over competitors.

Part of the key shift of resources must be to increase the proportion of the defence budget which we spend on R&D,[12] and to improve our ability to harness all the intellectual assets within our control so as to make better use of them and to enable them better to tap into our civilian assets.[13] This is the only way we will have the capacity to produce our own equipment to meet our own requirements if and when we need them, and to buy appropriate equipment from the world market.

The importance of 'generations' in the acquisition of capability

Acquisition has to support what may be described as a three 'generations' of capability concurrently: the current generation of forces that provide our 'readiness' to conduct current campaigns; the next generation of potential forces, exploring how to conduct campaigns in the forecastable future; and exploration of future capabilities. The foundation for all three is a healthy research community stimulated by open-source intelligence.

This generational model allows the investment made to be assessed against the values anticipated and realised. It is not designed to enable changing the whole capability on a given date. The generations have different time-constants and their implementation is designed to be staggered. The difficulty of managing this is not appreciated by the critics of MoD, and their imposition of simplistic solutions has amplified the problems of creating our arsenal with a relatively constant budget that is insufficient to meet all our aspirations. Other national-scale investments suffer similar difficulties, and it is time that government/parliament sponsored research to address the matter. The solutions open to commerce and industry do not apply to security matters or infrastructure projects, *viz*. the recent outcry over Network Rail improving the lines into Euston, or the electricity supply problems.

The R&D statistics from SET allow the Frascati categories to be identified for defence. They show an alarming reduction in Applied Strategic Research from £196m in 2001-02 to £3m in 2012-13, in constant 2012 prices. Specific Research appears to have been protected since it has a broadly flat profile over this period, while experimental development has roughly halved from £2bn to £0.9bn. This raises questions about MoD's strategy, rather than its processes. The senior management have effectively stopped all research on third generation capability by the reduction in strategic research. Such a dramatic reduction in experimental development means that they can have no plans to introduce significant improvements in the capability of the next generation systems. This appears to contradict their own published strategies. While it is possible that this is to exaggerate the situation, these figures do nothing to suggest that the leadership of MoD understands the importance of sustaining investment across three generations concurrently.

Adaptable forces

Forces cannot be created instantaneously, nor can equipment or services. Hence it is vital that MoD has sufficient intelligence – in both senses of the word – to generate appropriate forces in time. This requires MoD to have a structure centred on the task of identifying future commitments, to integrate the open and closed Intelligence, to consider its implications and match the powers needed to the opportunities or threats. Intelligence on world-wide research and development provides the opportunity to exploit this for our purposes, and to identify longer term potential instabilities that should shape our grand strategy and our research and equipment programmes.[14]

A reduced budget also means that we need to choose more carefully what equipment we try to adapt or invent. We will need to be able to reduce the proportion of our equipment that is specially made and concentrate more on what we can buy when we need it, adapting this for the required purpose at the time. This is different from buying 'off the shelf', which is a misplaced means of attempting to avoid R&D costs. The risk with 'off the shelf' purchasing is that we buy the wrong equipment, without owning the intellectual property to allow us to adapt it to suit a particular campaign, and without the guarantee of support (spares, software codes, etc.) to sustain it.

It is also dangerous to maintain a high proportion of the equipment budget in platforms at the expense of investment in weapons systems. Modularised weapons can be retro-fitted cheaply and very effectively to a variety of platforms. This is most obvious in the Royal Navy, which can benefit dramatically from this cost-

Table 1-1: Frascati Analysis

Constant 2012 prices (£ millions)		2001-2002	2002-2003	2003-2004	2004-2005	2005-2006	2006-2007	2007-2008	2008-2009	2009-2010	2010-2011	2011-2012	2012-2013
Applied Strategic Research		196	161	161	91	36	40	23	14	31	22	17	3
	%R	27.1%	24.6%	24.7%	11.8%	5.1%	5.5%	3.2%	2.2%	5.0%	4.0%	3.0%	0.5%
	%R&D	7.3%	4.6%	6.1%	3.4%	1.3%	1.6%	1.0%	0.6%	1.7%	1.2%	1.3%	0.2%
Applied Specific Research		527	494	492	683	676	692	693	627	583	534	545	562
	%R	72.9%	75.4%	75.3%	88.2%	94.9%	94.5%	96.8%	97.8%	95.0%	96.0%	97.0%	99.5%
	%R&D	19.7%	14.2%	18.5%	25.7%	25.3%	28.2%	28.7%	28.7%	31.1%	30.3%	41.0%	38.5%
Total Research		723	655	653	774	712	732	716	641	614	556	562	565
Experimental development	%R&D	1,949	2,817	2,004	1,882	1,959	1,726	1,698	1,544	1,257	1,207	766	895
		72.9%	81.1%	75.4%	70.9%	73.3%	70.2%	70.3%	70.7%	67.1%	68.5%	57.6%	61.3%
TOTAL		2,673	3,472	2,657	2,656	2,671	2,458	2,415	2,185	1,872	1,763	1,329	1,460
Deflator		77.0	78.8	80.3	82.5	84.0	86.4	88.6	91.1	93.6	96.0	98.3	100.0

effective wartime procedure in today's time of rapid change. This approach will encourage investment where it is most effective for wartime agile capability, influence and deterrence. This includes a renewed focus on our maritime presence in peacetime as an instrument for non-provocative influence and deterrence. The seas are the best medium for passive deterrence, particularly for a maritime trading nation with global interests, like the UK. But, to do this, we need to adapt our maritime strategic concept; for more platforms at a much lower cost. This would meet our ambition to avoid 'strategic shrinkage' while spending less on defence.

The future capabilities and capacities we will need are just as likely to be *services*, with people as their main component – think *intelligence* or *cyber*. Despite living in a technological age, or rather because of it, more than ever people remain the key force multiplier in any modern conflict. Investing in people, their skills, technological creativity and their ability to adapt and lead, is the most important component of defence spending. These people are not just armed servicemen and women; they are scientists, researchers, manufacturers and inventors throughout the UK economy.

We do not want to preserve or rebuild the old armed forces we had; we want to build new, relevant forces which will be different in concept and in the way different elements interact with each other and with the wider defence and security community.

A new business model: different leadership

MOD's acquisition management methods must reflect the needs of acquisition, which cannot be captured or led by the old idea of 'performance management'. This is not to denigrate assessment and measurement of personal and group performance. But creativity and energy will not be released by the self-defeating practice of reducing relationships to nothing more than targets, contracts and financial punishment or reward. The best people need inspiring and mentoring. Effective leadership assesses how people approach their tasks and working relationships, not simply what they produce. Such leadership must transcend public and private sectors.

The reduction in our acquisition budget now requires new forms of partnership involving government, industry, commerce and academe to generate the systems needed. Successful relationships will depend less on contracts and incentives and much more on mutually agreed goals and aspirations, which in turn will depend upon trust and shared values, rather than on the institutional conflict between government and industry which characterises today's system.

Today's concept of defence 'prime contractors' is no longer fit for purpose, as the volume of equipment we are now acquiring is too small. This means the MoD needs to develop the capacity to create and sustain many more constructive relationships with suppliers. The UK Trade & Industry Defence Services Organisation (UKTI DSO) should be part of such networks to restore our competitive stance.

Since we must move towards an adaptive military model, we need networks of companies that can produce quickly and in relatively small quantities what is needed for a campaign. We should be developing the networks of smaller companies that can do this. This is one of our British national traits, which we should be exploiting to our competitive advantage. Using networks of small companies will stimulate our intellectual capability and grow the economy in a way that subsidising the prime contractors' monopoly will never do. This is why the merger of EADS (now Airbus) and BAE was such a flawed concept, because it would have led UK defence in diametrically the opposite direction.

This brings us back again to a point made above: that the first requirement is to rebuild a research programme funded across the board at a national level. Without this we will not be able to produce anything special which will give us an edge, or which others will want to buy. While the MoD's current R&D budget is derisory as a proportion of our defence industry and must be increased, we need also to harness civilian R&D assets[15] to this end in conjunction with defence R&D. Any increase in defence spending should be directed to this end rather than for new equipment programmes. For example, the development of a UK drone programme is far better value than a purchase programme that does not build R&D capacity for the future.

If we are going to maintain a national arsenal, then we need to find a different model of arsenal, given the limitations on our defence budget, of our R&D and of our defence industry in today's service sector-dominated economy. The only arsenal that makes sense is one which can be generated mainly from non-defence parts of our national economy. We must be better able to create our military and security capability and capacity from a prototyping civilian-based economy, designing and making weapons based on civilian processes and using civilian capacity. To do this effectively, we need to understand what the UK as a whole, rather than simply its defence industry, is capable of generating. Many of the equipment products and services will have value across several of the campaigns we need to undertake, particularly if designed using modularity and commonality where this does not impose penalties and warrants similar unit costs. These common products and services should form part of our *core* acquisition programme, along with the long lead-time equipment needed for our nuclear deterrence. Additional equipment and services may need to be included in this new 'arsenal', developed to the prototype stage. For these infrequent acquisitions, we will need to retain design teams and to refine the manufacturing techniques and plant needed for rapid acquisition. The core is there to be expanded to meet the needs of campaigns and to be contracted when the campaign is ended and when reconstitution /regeneration/replacement are required: we cannot fight old wars better, new wars will be *different*.

National strategy or 'grand strategy'

A conscious formulation of strategy is essential if we are to rethink what we do with our capabilities. Often it is better to have a presence somewhere in the world rather than to have to fire a shot in anger. As Sun Tzu suggests, the prime purpose of the armed forces is not to fight, but to influence.

This means giving stronger and more careful recognition to the validity of the concept of 'national interests'.[16] The government must accept that the UK should have more concrete grand strategy and must understand the importance of adopting a national competitive stance so as to be able to campaign for our place in the world we inhabit. This does not mean being tied to a particular plan. Defence reviews have always purported to be strategic, but they are not a fixed plan. A strong and agile military capability (people, technology and equipment) is available to conduct (peaceful) campaigns to support foreign policy objectives and to influence the strategic environment. The choice is not between the 'foreign adventures' of recent decades and believing instead that the UK is in decline and should accept this fact. This is a false choice: it reflects the mind-set of declinism, which must be confronted. Defence and security are not luxuries, but a necessity for national survival. Defence will not represent good value for the UK unless it understands its strategic context, and unless that in turn reflects what our country represents in the world.

The next SDSR

The next SDSR must therefore be a genuine security review, considering defence and security in the round, rather than simply another cost-based review of our defence programmes. The review needs to connect our security priorities to our interests and our values by considering such fundamental questions as:

- who are we as a nation?
- what is in our national interest?
- what kind of country do we want to be?

To that extent, the so called National Security Strategy should also be formulated as a 'review', and titled as such. The next SDSR needs to answer two big questions:

1. How, in the light of the current financial climate, the turmoil of the on-going defence reform process, the buying up of our industrial capacity

by foreign firms, the loss of technical expertise in MoD and the lack of technically competent leadership, does the UK preserve the *ownership of the acquisition process?*

2. How do we build and preserve the *infrastructure of acquisition* which we will need to generate a new, adaptable force, rather than the inventory created by it? We need to preserve and develop the necessary understanding and ability to lead and sustain the acquisition structure within MOD. This cannot be outsourced.

If we are to succeed in building truly relevant defence forces, we therefore need two things in particular which are currently outside our Armed Forces' power to deliver. These are:

(a) An agile and adaptable acquisition system able to deliver both equipment and services rapidly and as needed to enable a wide range of kinetic and non-kinetic campaigns

(b) A new funding mechanism from the Treasury to enable this to happen

Urgent operational requirements

There are numerous successful examples of the UK meeting its urgent operational requirements when faced with an immediate need. Indeed MoD has repeatedly invented agile acquisition systems to sustain all major campaigns. This model is appropriate to products and services that can be delivered within the operational time constants. Given the environment we face, it could be argued that this should be the basic acquisition model, augmented by variants that address the long-time constants of existential deterrence.

Acquisition culture

The complexity of acquisition makes it difficult to find solutions sufficiently simple to be politically advocated or for non-specialists to understand easily. We have chosen to use the term 'culture' as a way of explaining the complex network of interacting influences, outlined below, which in no small measure determine whether or not it will be possible to establish an effective acquisition system. Acquisition *culture* is taken to mean the grand strategy shared by the security community, which includes the acquisition community.

We have clustered the influences into three coupled sets:

1. **Philosophy:** the philosophy underpinning our grand strategy depends on our assessment of the instabilities (conflicts, problems, natural disasters etc.) that we have or expect to face; on the values that underpin our interests; on the campaigning we undertake, with its associated complexity, networks and the need for agility; and on the impact of our current smallness, the available arsenals, the abilities of the security community.

2. **Practice:** the delivery of grand strategy depends on intelligence, research, education, training; and on the fitness of governance, the role and competence of parliament, the appropriateness of funding mechanisms and the capabilities and capacity we invest in.

3. **Self adaptation:** ensures that our acquisition can evolve to become and remain fit-for-purpose and, in its turn, help the security community to learn to adapt, stimulating change by investing in education and by recognising the community, challenging them rather than berating them.

Conclusion

What would a successful transformation of defence acquisition look like? The outcome of a new approach to defence acquisition would be to concentrate on three things.

- Firstly, on developing defence know-how, and a research and industrial base from within and beyond government, which can develop new technologies and techniques, as and when the demand arises to serve the foreign and security campaigns of the day.

- Secondly, to evolve away from the idea of big defence equipment programmes, dependent upon the very few defence prime contractors. This means thinking about much cheaper and more numerous weapons platforms, but capable of being adapted to carry weapons systems suitable for the task.

- Thirdly, to use money to invest in smaller and medium-sized enterprises and their research and development programmes, working in collaboration with government, so that they can generate the weapons systems required for specific campaigns, rather than for standing capability.

This would place the MoD more on a permanent agile 'war footing', ready and adaptable, and fitted for the unpredictable world in which we now live.

Bernard Jenkin, Chris Donnelly and David McOwat

1

Understanding the Challenge

Bernard Jenkin, Chris Donnelly and David McOwat

1.1. Introduction

This paper is being written in a period of great turbulence in our national governance and in international affairs, driven by the huge increase in world population and global interconnectedness. Our governance is evolving rapidly in an attempt to make it fit for purpose. Meanwhile, our economy and financial institutions have not yet recovered from the market bubbles, and we show no signs of rediscovering our competitive stance in developing a grand strategy.

Our security is threatened by this turbulence, but we have yet to see any significant evolution in our means of providing security. The essential recognition of the complexity of security, shown by the creation of the National Security Council, has not yet produced a meaningful means of co-ordinating parliament, government, the civil, diplomatic and military services, industry, commerce, and our educational and academic institutions in a grand strategy.

Acquisition is a fundamental component of our competitive stance. It is central to delivery of all government services, but is most visible in defence, as evidenced by the almost perpetual criticisms of and changes to defence acquisition. None of these changes have succeeded. This suggests that they are on the wrong evolutionary trajectory and need a new direction, rather than improvements. Acquisition failures empower opponents, since they recognise a weakness, and they weaken allies, who doubt our ability to contribute when required. Acquisition is therefore a highly visible component of deterrence and stability.

This report, then, is not another silver bullet, written by the outsiders, the retired with time on their hands, or those with an agenda. It is an attempt to stimulate a rapid evolution of the acquisition process by those charged with its delivery. This work is not a set of solutions, but it does propose ideas to stimulate this evolutionary leap. These ideas will, no doubt, not all be right. But perhaps they will be less wrong than the current approach. Neither is this work an attempt to apportion blame, but rather to encourage a creative, learning culture within the community responsible for our security.

Aim

The aims of this study are (a) to consider what the principles of acquisition are for the UK's security in the early twenty-first Century, and (b) how we can create a healthy culture that enables our acquisition processes to evolve continuously and be fit for purpose in the future.

Scope

Acquisition for defence and security is a large and truly complex problem. It cannot be reduced to a simple, short brief, nor is it amenable to the most fashionable managerial panaceas from external consultants, as the recent failure of the GOGO proposal demonstrates. These panaceas have been applied in profusion over the last 25 years to no apparent advantage. The most difficult question of defence policy is choosing what we need to have today in order to be ready for what we cannot anticipate. This cannot be contracted out. This study is an attempt to draw out some of the basic principles and avoid the pitfalls of oversimplification or tunnel vision.

National security is 'managed' by government, but accountable to parliament on behalf of those whom MPs represent: the UK population – the real 'owner'. This study, therefore, also addresses parliament and people, rather than just the managers, with proposals to help create a healthy culture within which acquisition can evolve. The first requirement is to make acquisition fit for purpose once again. The subsequent requirement is to create the capacity for acquisition to evolve continuously in response to the changing circumstances, under a suitable form of governance and funding.

1.2. Not just another solution to MoD's acquisition failures

Since 2010, the coalition brought some welcome discipline and stability to defence procurement. However, merely making the wrong acquisition concept work better will not provide the best outcome. It is now widely recognised that there is a fundamental lack of fitness in our acquisition capacity and capability. Numerous studies, reports and parliamentary inquiries have sought to analyse the reasons and propose solutions, frequently pillorying MoD in the process. This study is *not* another such 'solution'.

MoD certainly bears some responsibility for the failure of its acquisition processes, but it is not just a problem of MoD; and MoD alone cannot solve the acquisition problem. What is not widely understood is that our acquisition problem is not the result of particular system failures in MOD: any healthy organisation in tune with its environment would have adapted, as MoD has done successfully many times in the past. The failure is wider and more complex. We need to consider how to travel a different evolutionary trajectory if we are to regain MoD's fitness-for-purpose and rebuild a healthy acquisition capability and capacity.

As we noted above, defence and security acquisition is fundamental to our national security. It contributes to advancing UK interests by providing the equipment and services needed to deter and counter threats and to create or to exploit opportunities. It underpins our defence and deterrence postures and, through this, much of our leading-edge industrial and commercial competitiveness. In a globalised world, the suppliers of the equipment and services can no longer all be UK-owned or even UK-based organisations. It is therefore essential to identify which assets must remain under national ownership and control. National industrial and commercial power is a key part of our national security.

Acquisition is coupled to the global security environment. But it is based on the intellectual abilities, attitudes and personal qualities of the people involved; on the health of the institutions within which they work; and on the effectiveness of the procedures they employ. Acquisition, therefore, unites academe, governance and statecraft, industry, commerce and our security sector in an indivisible, complex *partnership*. This in turn requires exceptional leadership, which not only comprehends the scale and complexity of defence acquisition, but understands that defence acquisition depends on sharing a sense of mission, and on a high level of trust and agreement about fundamental values.

Acquisition is not just about the process of buying military hardware. Acquiring capabilities and capacities involves all aspects of our national political, economic and social systems. It is fundamental to our *competitive stance* in the world, and to the effectiveness and survival of our armed forces personnel.

Acquisition is one of the principal competencies of government and parliament, experienced by the public in the delivery of the products and services they expect from their political leaders. Acquisition is therefore often politicised, in a party or individual sense. This is inevitable, so the people and institutions involved must be able to cope with this additional challenge.

1.3 Understanding defence acquisition within today's political and economic environment

Let us assume that government will decide that, henceforth, the UK is going to limit its defence budget to two per cent of GDP. This demands a new grand strategy to ensure our national security. Those who do not believe in grand strategy and who assert that all the government needs is 'pragmatism' to react to events are living in a past age when our defence budget was double or treble today's two per cent. At two per cent, we are spending so little that we need to think and plan very carefully to be sure that we are spending wisely.

We cannot 'insure' ourselves against all threats with such a small budget. Consequently we have to start understanding the defence budget as investment, and look to where it will yield the best returns.

Given that the costs of major weapon systems rise at a defence inflation rate of up to eight per cent above the general rate of inflation,[1] a grand strategy reflecting a defence budget of two per cent of GDP cannot be based on acquiring the ability to generate power that is dominated by equipment. We need to invent on a regular basis new system concepts with a lower cost base, rather than refine and inflate the costs of existing concepts. It is more and more important that we acquire the right equipment, and acquire it well, because we can afford so little of it. But the acquisition of ever more expensive military equipment must not be allowed to get in the way of our acquiring the other forms of power which we will need to deal with the threats and problems of the twenty-first century. Similarly, we may have to consider new ways of retaining a sufficient arsenal to respond to unforeseen instabilities.

In his supporting essay David McOwat tentatively identifies five categories of challenges or problems we are likely to face in the coming years, each of which brings threats and opportunities. No one acquisition strategy will cope with all five categories. The challenges are radically different and what we must acquire, if we are to cope with them, is accordingly subject to different demands. The most significant of these is the different time-scale that each category of challenge brings with it.

The existential threat, for example, requires us to acquire and to maintain the deterrent force, at the core of which is our nuclear capability. This necessitates very long-term equipment programmes indeed, which are anything but agile and cannot easily be changed, even at vast expense. By contrast, the acquisition timescales for other threats can be very short. It is the timescales which, more than any other factor, will determine, in each case: the acquisition strategy; the form of funding; the management style; and the authority which is needed to ensure that we can acquire what we need, when we need it, to deal with a specific threat. Daily 'hypercompetition' may be a less obvious danger to our nation than invasion or nuclear attack, but it is just as serious a threat and may consume much of the investment.

Key to ensuring our national sovereignty when it comes to acquiring the capability and capacity to deal with threats to our security is to recognise and sustain a UK identity. Identity is a complex issue and is dealt with later in this volume. At its heart is governance. Our five-year electoral cycle means that grand strategy cannot be owned by government alone. Each successive government is the temporary custodian of our national grand strategy, responsible for its tactical management. In past times our strong, technically competent, depoliticised civil service guaranteed much of the long-term perspective. But that civil service has now largely gone and a new long-term guarantor must be found. At the moment, only parliament could step up to fill this gap, just as Congress does in the USA. This is an issue that we must face up to as a matter of urgency. At the moment, parliament does not do this, though it has the potential.

In past times, much was made of defence 'spin-off', i.e. the benefits brought to other areas of UK life by defence spending. But on a budget of two per cent of GDP, the opposite is now the case. Today, defence must be able to exploit our national civilian research, education, commercial and industrial strategies because, with a budget of two per cent of GDP, defence can no longer replace or determine these other strategies. Defence must now influence them to ensure that they take account of defence needs and are amended accordingly. We need defence 'spin-in'. The MoD/Research Councils joint research programme used to ensure that some of the postgraduate and post-doctorate academic research was relevant to defence needs. This programme has withered. Similarly, MoD representation on the Engineering Sciences Research Councils has diminished, and this means of supporting interesting research has also been eliminated. Only with determined and sustained efforts will we be able to reverse this trend.

Similarly, the UK now needs to take a leaf out of China's book and start systematically to hoover up and exploit knowledge from the rest of the world, as our investment in defence R&D is now too small to support the range of innovation required to meet our challenges. China's 'open source' intelligence process provides a good model, but there are several others of note we could emulate.

Alliances must also be managed for our national benefit. At the moment, they are not so managed and concepts of our 'national benefit' tend to be uncertain, subjective and ill-defined. In our alliance with the US, the UK is definitely a junior partner. Within NATO, the UK seems to contribute more than it benefits. European members of NATO see very different threats, depending on where they are situated - something which will need a lot of investment of time and effort on our part to reconcile, if NATO is to remain effective and contribute to our security, rather than be a drain on our assets. Our (security) alliance with the EU is simply not serious, other than with France, where we blow hot and cold.

When it comes to equipment acquisition, this all gets very awkward. Our allies, including the US, have consistently sought to diminish our national defence industry in their own interest, to do away with competition. Other countries have chosen to protect their national industry more than the UK, which has sold much of its national technical capabilities, not to mention strategic infrastructure, to foreign firms that have no interest in the maintenance of national capacity. The comfortable assumption that we will be able to buy what we need from abroad when we need it is not backed up by any serious analysis. We need to do a lot of work to understand what forms of power (kinetic and non-kinetic) we might need to generate in future conflicts; what we can make and what we will need to buy in, and from where; and what to do if it is not available on the day.

Scale is another issue we must now rethink at two per cent. The case for huge, monopoly prime contractors can no longer be convincingly made, except possibly for very long-timescale 'existential threat' programmes; and even there they are looking increasingly anachronistic. Small is beautiful. If we are no longer acquiring for industrial-scale war, we need new models of agility and adaptability. The UK's world-beating Formula 1 motor industry may supply just such a model and is worthy of closer scrutiny. How is it that Norway can keep over 100 shipyards working, whereas the UK has only a handful? Reliance on a private national prime contractor to maintain our national core competencies has clearly not worked. Our defence industrial spending now runs at about two-thirds of one per cent of GDP. The defence industry doubles this with export sales, but they are largely based on aircraft and other equipment designed decades ago and which we no longer have the pipeline to replace. What happens when the present product lifecycle comes to an end? What alternatives to prime contractors can we adopt which will give a better return on our investment? From whom can we learn?

This brings us back to the governance question. Defence needs a grand strategy, which needs some new, or rather rediscovered, politics. Defence and grand strategy should not be issues of competition between political parties: that cannot be in the national interest. Details should be debated but within an overall umbrella of an agreed grand strategy. This already is the case to some degree (for example, the consensus among the main parties about the maintenance of the nuclear deterrent), but a more overt and openly expressed cross-party approach would totally change the discussion and debate and move it from addressing efficiency and costs to addressing effectiveness and values. This is the revolution to which this study can, we hope, make a small contribution.

1.4. Overcoming Declinism: How Not to Treat Acquisition

The UK security community must learn to expand and contract in response to the changing security environment. During periods of reduction there is danger that the immense strategic management challenges slip into *declinism*,[2] rather than creating a different, smaller capacity matched to the new environment. The volume of criticism levelled against MoD, ministers and industry suggests that this is, in fact, what has occurred during the dramatic reduction from some eight per cent of GDP spent on defence at the height of the Cold War to today's two per cent of GDP. The rush to claim credit for identifying solutions to the acquisition problems that have arisen as budgets have shrunk (usually from people with no responsibility for the implementation of those solutions) has exacerbated the problems rather than solved them. These 'solutions' merely cause high quality, highly motivated people to tire of the uninformed criticism, so that the system appears incapable of self-correction.

This is no way to treat a matter of such strategic importance as acquisition. Irresponsible criticism of acquisition attacks the UK's interests and lowers the value of our investment in security. This is not to excuse MoD or any other part of the security community from responsibility; but we must provide an environment for constructive criticism that improves acquisition. If the nation is going to invest only two per cent of GDP in its defence, then there is every reason to ensure that the investment is relevant and delivers maximum value, balanced between deterring or combatting threats and exploiting opportunities. Although the equipment budget amounts to less than one per cent of GDP, this investment has a disproportionate impact because much of it stimulates the science and engineering base used by civil industry and challenges academic research fields, particularly in cross-disciplinary topics such as socio-technical systems. We have lost sight of this issue and allowed our science and engineering base to decline. This is an example of *declinism* in action.

It has become clear that the environment within which the

MoD and its acquisition processes are operating is changing so rapidly, and has changed in a way which is so hostile to the functioning of the MoD, that, unless the acquisition environment itself is improved, no amount of effort put in by MoD will produce a solution to the acquisition problem.

From this perspective, addressing – or rather, attacking – the people and processes of the MoD as the sole cause of the acquisition problem is likely to make the problem worse, rather than identify real solutions. The intellect, skills, attitude and behaviour of the people involved in the acquisition process are more important factors in determining success than are the structure and organisations involved. If we cannot motivate and improve the morale of the people engaged in the current acquisition community, we shall suffer a strategic failure every bit as large as losing any war, for we will have no effective acquisition and, without that, we can have no security. Without resources, we have no capacity to advance our interests, just as without the right people we have no effective armed forces, no matter how good our equipment.

2

The Principles of Acquisition

2.1. What is acquisition?

2.1.1. Acquisition as a strategic capacity

In addressing this topic, vocabulary is very important, and a lot of our current problems have arisen because of confusion between the terms *purchasing, procurement* and *acquisition*.

Purchasing is buying equipment or services that are (or are nearly) available off-the-shelf. This is wrongly viewed as the simplest acquisition form; but it brings with it different and no less demanding challenges. The buyer is a *customer* and will likely have alternatives to choose between from a range of suppliers in some form of market. (This was referred to as 'Ordinary Customer Status' in the past.) A lot of what we buy for defence falls into this category of 'commodity'. As long as we have competent defence and acquisition communities that can identify what we need and know what can be bought, then the extra skills needed for effective and efficient purchasing are hard-nosed *commercial* skills independent of defence. However, commercial skills must be augmented by those of the user and technical communities: expertise in developing novel concepts of operation and methods to assess the suitability of competing solutions are both vital in identifying a requirement and in identifying effective uses for equipment or services available from the market place. *Procurement* is buying equipment or services to fit within a known equipment or service concept, which need modifying or developing from scratch – a small proportion might even need to be unique. The buyer, therefore, is actually a *client*, as he must work *with* the supplier in a relationship that needs nurturing if it is to be successful. This was previously referred to as 'Intelligent Customer Status', but also included the small volume associated with 'Expert Customer Status'.

Whereas *purchasing* demands a *commercial* skills base, *procurement* demands a *technical* skills base. This is because the greatest uncertainty and compromise concern the performance of the kit or service, which is a complex technical matter, not solely a commercial issue. The risk is technical in nature, and the decisions between client and supplier are technical, not financial, e.g. what is it that we can't do? What is the best way to get round the problem? To talk about a problem in *procurement*, as opposed to *purchasing*, as being caused by 'a badly drawn-up contract' is evidence of *technical* ignorance.

As the procurement progresses, the buyer is likely to have to modify his needs to accommodate time, technical or budgetary constraints; this requires both military and technical expertise. The suppliers may have to modify what is produced, based on the best they can do within the constraints. This requires trust as well as a high level of technical competence, hence the need to nurture the relationship. The research and development budgets also have to be adjustable to cope with the technical needs of the project as it develops.

It is when the decision timetable is fixed for administrative convenience, rather than driven by operational needs, or when the decision to proceed without adaptation is taken without adequate information because of financial regulations, that problems usually ensue. Managing all this requires appropriate processes as well as specific skills in those charged with its oversight.

This category, i.e. *procurement*, is seen to be the heart of the acquisition programme. With the wisdom of hindsight, we can see that our problems in this area were made worse, first, by the move of the procurement executive from London to Bristol, causing some 50 per cent of our technical experts to resign; secondly, by the closure of DERA; thirdly, as the armed forces shrank, by the drying-up of the input of technical military experts, who had set the standard on what could be accepted in terms of performance of the product. At the same time, the MoD cut down on deploying its technical experts into the industrial producers. Their job had been to disseminate knowledge, but they had also acted as the MoD's 'facilitators' in industry, contributing to the atmosphere of understanding and trust.

These events soon stopped the supply of technical expertise into the acquisition community and destroyed the career structure within that community. Replacing this technical expertise with 'project management' completed the destruction. A procurement project is, by definition, technical. It cannot be managed without technical, military and commercial expertise at all levels. Without technical expertise, it is impossible to build the necessary relationship between client and supplier. However, this interpretation is not currently shared by the Cabinet Office Government Procurement Service Agency.

Acquisition includes purchasing and procurement, but is more than that. It involves knowing the whole life-cycle of the set of capabilities and associated capacity we need. It means understanding why we need it, and the best means of delivery, employment, support and disposal (i.e. what to mothball, what to move to the reserves, what to discard, and how). Acquisition, therefore, requires not only a high degree of technical expertise, but very wide-ranging expertise encompassing *all* the range of powers we need to generate, not only the kinetic, and encompassing not just industry, but all relevant areas of our society and economy on which acquisition will depend.

Acquisition is an important part of our overall strategic capacity. As such, it involves several clients and indeed multiple ministries, as it must address the UK national interests, not just those of a particular community. As a strategic asset, therefore, acquisition is assessed in *global value to UK Interests*. Purchasing and procurement, by contrast, can be assessed in *local* values. Assessing value is an outstanding research problem, it seems, for we have found no indication of its use anywhere in government. The Treasury metrics are only relevant to simple systems, so may be appropriate to purchasing *costs*, but they offer no help in addressing how to make larger, coupled *value* judgements.

Acquisition as a strategic capability in its own right is most evident when the very existence of the equipment is part of its capability, that is, when our opponent is not sure if we possess something – or, if we do, what it can do – unless we choose to demonstrate its effect. Nuclear weapons, electronic or cyber warfare, encryption and decoding are all good examples. These are things we must have under national control, which means we must control all aspects of their manufacture and use, including people trained in their use and the intellectual property. This is not compatible with foreign ownership or a commercial operator. An analogous issue arises in equipment and services that must evolve more rapidly than those of an opponent during a campaign so as to ensure campaign success. Acquisition capacity, therefore, affects the concepts of operations and the campaign plan.

This is a wider view of acquisition than is included in the new MoD operating model.[1] However, this appears to be a highly simplified representation of how MoD works. It is hoped that the real model is more realistic and adaptable.

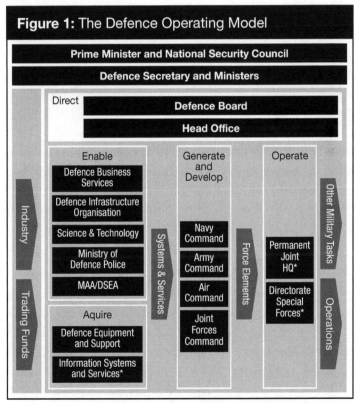

Figure 1: The Defence Operating Model

Source: MoD, 'How Defence Works', 2014, p4

2.1.2 Acquisition viewed through the lens of ecology

In most studies of acquisition failure, the relationship between MoD, government, parliament and people is ignored, as the wider social, political and economic factors in today's UK are similarly ignored. The assumption that acquisition failure is simply a systems failure within MoD leads to the search for culprits on whom to pin the blame, and for panaceas – 'silver bullets' – which will provide a quick, permanent solution and bring kudos to the proponent. The proposition of this study is that acquisition can only be understood, and effective acquisition processes established, if the world in which we are striving to ensure our national security is viewed through *ecology*, i.e. a constantly changing environment with many competing and co-operating entities embedded within it.

In ecology there are the *actors* – for Darwin, the animals; for us, the active states, institutions and other groups (e.g. non-state actors) – and there is the *environment*. The actors are in constant interaction – competition and/or cooperation – with each other, but also within and with their environment. This environment constantly changes, but the nature and rate of change can vary widely over time and the actors themselves can contribute to this change, consciously or unconsciously, and sometimes dramatically. As Darwin pointed out, it is not strength or size, which, in the long term, determines whether a species survives: it is the ability to adapt to remain fitted to its environment and to cope with the challenge from its competitors. In our case, this is true of our defence and security institutions and of our acquisition processes.

We can advance our interests by (a) seeking (asymmetric) advantage over our competitors directly or through a network of competitors and collaborators, and (b) influencing the environment. Globalisation is sufficiently advanced that we are already subject to extreme competitive pressures, whether we recognize them or not.

Forces cannot be created instantaneously, nor equipment or services. Hence it is vital that MoD has sufficient intelligence – in both senses of the word – to generate appropriate forces in time. This requires MoD to have a structure centred on the task of identifying future commitments, to integrate the open and closed Intelligence, to consider its implications and match the powers needed to the opportunities or threats. Intelligence on world research and development provides the opportunity to exploit it for our purposes, and to identify longer term instabilities that should shape our grand strategy and our research and equipment programmes.[2]

2.2. Acquisition in grand strategy: rediscovering the competitive stance

2.2.1 Values and interests

What are the interests of the UK that we hope to advance? What values underpin them? The assessment of the worth of acquisition programmes arises from the answers to these questions. Who today stops to consider these questions? Who in government or in parliament is responsible for ensuring these questions are answered? Everyone assumes that the answers are known, but by someone else. In fact, many of our current equipment programmes are based on the absence of answers, so that decisions are based on obsolete ideas and unsubstantiated requirements.

The questions about interests and values go to the heart of what sort of country we want to be and how we see our place in the world. For example, Tony Blair attempted to address this when he set out the doctrine of humanitarian intervention in his Chicago speech of 1999.[3] As he found, the greatest difficulty appears to lie in agreeing a set of values and interests that are sufficiently general to be shared by the greater part, if not all, of the population, rather than a particular group or party. At a time when we are questioning our membership of the European Union; whether Scotland should be part of the UK; or whether the UK constitution should be reformulated in a federal form; or whether we are an active player in global security or not, the underpinnings of consensus about acquisition strategy are very uncertain. All these issues need to be resolved as soon as possible. How should acquisition evolve in the light of this uncertainty?

Acquisition for defence and security can involve timelines much longer than an election cycle. This raises the issue of 'ownership' of security and acquisition strategy. There has always been a strong desire for consensus and a willingness of leaders of all political parties to work together in matters of defence and security, even where fundamental disagreements about military operations or capabilities (e.g. nuclear) have existed. The rise in the importance of select committees (particularly Defence, Foreign Affairs, Treasury, Public Accounts and Public Administration) and the establishment of the joint National Security Committee represent further steps towards developing parliament as the ultimate owner and supervisor of security and acquisition strategy, which transcends party and elections.

We now need to give further thought to the question of how select committees and parliament as a whole can generate and sustain support in government and explain a more coherent UK national strategy so that government departments and industry better understand what the political leadership is seeking to achieve and why.

2.2.2 Intelligence

Next, we need to assess what threats, challenges and opportunities we are facing and will face as we strive to advance our interests: which challenges we will deal with by deterrence or prevention, which by engagement; which opportunities we will create and which will we exploit. Only then can we establish what different forms of power — military and non-military — we must be able to generate to advance our interests, ensuring in the process that we can reduce our dependence on industrial warfare, which we know we can no longer afford. Only then can we create a sensible national strategy that interacts with industrial, commercial, educational and research strategies.

As noted previously, open-source intelligence contributes to developing our knowledge more widely than just within the narrow defence context. The huge growth in the world population of highly educated people means that that we must be able to identify and exploit *world* knowledge, not just that generated in the UK. Similarly, the domination of university research departments by high fee-earning, highly capable foreign students needs to be more-carefully considered with regard to its advantage to UK interests.

2.2.3 Campaigning

Campaigns, rather than *operations*, are the best way to approach deployments and tackle problems. There are different understandings of the term *campaign*. This is best expressed by the consideration that a military *operation* stops when the last bomb is dropped, as recently in Libya. But a *campaign* continues until the strategic objective is reached, in this case a healthy, prosperous, stable Libya – still a long way off.

If campaigning is going to be the basis of our interventions, we will need to create a strategic campaign plan to direct the campaign. This is a mix of the different forms of power that we can generate (acquire) in time, at a cost we can afford, in a system we can manage, sustain and replace. This is applicable for activities to *prevent* problems as well as for those in which an enemy is engaged. A campaign also needs a campaign infrastructure plan, including the acquisition of equipment, products and services, determining who is to provide what, and including intellectual services (e.g. information warfare).

At any particular time, the number of campaigns that we can support concurrently, and the nature of those campaigns, is limited by the capability and capacity that we have provided as part of our defence acquisition strategy. The question that national strategy has to address is the issue of capability versus capacity: what campaigns should we be planning for, and what and how many campaigns should we plan to support concurrently. This is far broader thinking than the current function of 'defence planning assumptions', which merely consider what military operations should be planned for.

2.3. Funding defence acquisition

2.3.1 The impact of economics[4]

In a world where we measure progress primarily in terms of increasing wealth (GDP) and technological advances, defence has a particular problem of cost inflation. Firstly, increasing wealth means higher and higher labour costs. In this environment, organisations that can reduce labour costs (e.g. by using computers and robots, or by outsourcing production to China, etc.) do well. But if an organisation must have people, then to cope with the rising cost of ever more highly skilled and better qualified people it must either have an increase in its budget or it will inevitably have to shrink or lose quality.

Secondly, technological advances tend to reduce the cost of equipment where that equipment can have a more or less stable level of performance. In real terms, TVs and washing machines get cheaper every year. But if the equipment needs to improve its performance significantly year on year because it is in lethal competition with an opponent, as in defence, the cost of the equipment will increase by about eight per cent per annum above the cost of inflation.[5] This reflects the higher cost base of the 'high-technology' component in the economy, where the costs of R&D and initial production are most apparent and production runs may be small. Much military equipment falls into this category. When the ever more costly equipment is not just used but consumed, and in quantity – as is the case with military equipment – the problem is exacerbated.

Thirdly, there is an added cost of defence equipment and services due to our having to match and excel the performance of commercial competitors so as to gain individual performance advantage. It is this which largely accounts for the constant high level of the defence equipment inflation rate.

Fourthly, there is the problem of 'overmatch', where we employ expensive systems against targets that do not need their performance level, because we have no appropriate systems or other form of power to employ. This is vastly wasteful, consuming expensive resources that should be retained for appropriate campaigns. Recent campaigns amply demonstrate this issue. For example, one of our five £1bn Dauntless class destroyers, with its PAAMS missile system and phased array radar, cannot deliver much value for money in counter insurgency or anti-piracy operations. Examples abound of our using expensive platforms and weapons, designed for the peer threat environment in Central Europe – MLRS, Storm Shadow, 2000lb PaveWay bombs – against the Taliban in Afghanistan; or the Royal Navy demonstrating its power by launching Tomahawk cruise missiles at every opportunity.

These four factors all hit defence hard. But they also affect the National Health Service, for reasons remarkably similar to defence: the 'evolving lethal competitor' is new strains of infection, coupled with an ever bigger and more vulnerable, ageing population which consumes ever more sophisticated drugs and services. However, governments seek to meet the cost of health inflation as an election-winner. They do not do so for defence inflation.

Our national strategy no longer includes preparing for industrial warfare typical of the twentieth century. Our acquisition process must recognise this and adapt accordingly. Over the last 20 years we have reduced our defence expenditure and the size of our armed forces considerably, but we have maintained the same organisational, manning and equipment model – a model which was designed for an armed forces of half a million and a budget well in excess of five per cent of GDP.

But, as we move to a defence budget of two per cent of GDP (or possibly even less), the model of defence that we still use breaks down. A process of reducing forces to support ever-smaller quantities of ever higher-performance equipment, plus the ever-increasing 'labour cost' of the soldiers, sailors and airmen and women trained to use this equipment, has brought us ever diminishing returns over the last 20 years, to the point at which defence today is no longer sustainable on this basis. The last SDSR failed to recognise this. Defence policy like this no longer has any credibility. We cannot meet today's challenges by another round of balanced reductions and incremental change. We need a new model for the next SDSR. The present cycle of force reductions requires us to change our fundamental organisational paradigm for defence and security, and therefore also for acquisition.

We are not the first country to face this problem. Most of our European allies reached this point of unsustainability a decade ago, did not recognise that they had to change radically, and now maintain forces that still cost a lot of 'bucks', but produce very little 'bang'. By contrast, in other parts of the world, faced with the same calculation, many of our rivals and opponents have chosen to refocus their rivalry and competition from classic military power to other 'weapons', for example: economic, political, cyber, bribery, corruption and information. They have worked out where their interests lie; they can think and act according to a coherent strategy. We need to be aware of this, aware that future conflict will not only be a matter of 'kinetics', and take account of it in our national strategy, our acquisition strategy, and in the next SDSR.

When it comes to contemplating radical change, we must recognise that we are all shaped by our personal and institutional experience, long-standing and cherished traditions, vested interests – and all the emotions that accompany these things. It is vital that we realise how, as a result, most of our current model of organisation and acquisition reflects the industrial society and mass industrialised wars of the twentieth century. We knew who the enemy would be and how the conflict would be fought and we organised ourselves to match that enemy, based on our industrial capacity.

Because of this experience, most people accept our current military system as 'normal'. They are just not aware of the extent to which our recent past has shaped our present military system and our perceptions of future conflict. It has become clear to us all that future war cannot be predicted, but it is unlikely to be a re-run of WWII, or the WWIII we expected. But our defence institutions, procedures and habits of mind do not yet reflect this reality. Our current acquisition system is geared to an industry we have lost. We can no longer replace by ourselves even the equipment we have used up on current operations.

The painful truth is that, as we have already noted, on two per cent of GDP, we can no longer maintain a 'robust' defence structure, i.e. organise and equip our forces to match all the potential opponents and cope with all the non-combat tasks they might face in the future. We must not fool ourselves that we can ignore this reality by relying on a technological advantage over a future enemy. Pretending that we had a meaningful technological advantage was often used to justify reducing our forces in the past. There might have been more truth in this when we had a highly-developed and effective R&D and corresponding industrial capability, when we could expect a war where platform matched platform and weapons matched weapons and the contest would be decided on that basis. But the most likely conflicts of today and tomorrow are primarily a clash of intellects and of systems, and also most often an asymmetric clash. We have been drawn in recent conflicts into using our weapons (and especially our platforms) in tasks for which they were never designed. It is an expensive waste – of equipment and manpower – which we cannot afford, and it does not confer the advantage we need. In Afghanistan, it has been estimated that it has cost the US $100m to kill each 'Taliban', and UK contributes to this ridiculous cost-per-kill figure, however questionable a metric it may be.

It is hard to face up to the implications of the UK's fundamental loss of capability and capacity. If a service sector-dominated state which spends only two per cent of its GDP on defence cannot have a 'robust' defence structure, then it must build a force for every campaign and not get into campaigns it cannot build for. This is what is meant by moving to an 'adaptable force', i.e. maintaining a military core on the basis of which forces appropriate to the (unforeseen) need can be generated quickly and effectively and reduced when the issue has been dealt with. This means we need an alternative to the system of committing money one year at a time and an understanding by the Treasury that they must invent a new, dynamic means of investing in security, recognising that it is not simply an insurance premium overhead or drain on the economy, or something with a twenty-five year cycle that allows 'time for adjustment'.

As we move to an adaptable force structure in the coming months and years it will have a revolutionary effect on our acquisition. Unfortunately, this reality has not yet been fully understood or acted upon in parliament, government, our defence establishment and industry.

2.3.2 Financing effective defence acquisition

We make no effort to identify, let alone manage, either the cost of security as a whole, or its value to the UK. The defence budget is not the total cost even of defence, let alone of security. MoD, like the other contributing Ministries, makes no effort to establish the value it contributes. We can find no studies by MoD of the appropriateness of the investment levels. This must be addressed if we are to decide whether the volume of national resources allocated to investment in security, and to defence in particular, is appropriate to advancing UK Interests or whether this level of investment is entirely arbitrary. What volume of investment in defence and security would best advance our interests or generate real value for money from the investment? How do we know that we are getting the best value out of two per cent of GDP? Would we get better value at 1.5 per cent or 2.5 per cent? If we do not know what we will need to do, i.e. which kind of threats or opportunities we will need to deal with, there is no frame of reference for making this assessment. We all know that the Treasury view of defence spending is 'the less, the better', and that somehow it is all 'a waste'.

Funding national security must be dynamic because we can no longer plan for a known threat as we did in the Cold War. As we have chosen not to have robustness as a strategy, because it is unaffordable, as we have already pointed out, we will have to build for (and build down after) each campaign. The current system of government finance is too short-term and does not provide the necessary continuity or certainty. This means we need new forms of financing for the security infrastructure. Attempts to engage private finance for funding defence infrastructure has proved more expensive than government finance, so efforts need to be concentrated on engaging the Treasury to develop new ways of financing defence and security. Private City expertise could be very useful here in helping to encourage flexibility, imagination and innovation at the Treasury. This underlines the fact that the intellectual capacity/capability to address any security or defence acquisition issue is just as important as the industrial, banking or diplomatic capability. This needs government, academia, the City and think tanks all to collaborate.

Furthermore, the current inadequate financing model, which prevents us funding projects with certainty and leads to underfunding, thereby injects cost and time performance penalties. Injecting ignorance = injecting cost, as ignorance = risk. This is compounded by inappropriate MoD management processes, including bringing in external experts or consultants who do not understand the relationships between operations, campaigns, capabilities and national strategy and who try to produce business-school solutions for letting and managing contracts, but which are about nothing else.

There will always be a problem if we cannot finance defence and acquisition properly: the Treasury will not let MoD act as a bank and provide investment when it is needed. It will be impossible to achieve agile acquisition unless defence funding is also agile. To address this problem, we need some sort of a defence (security) bank that can provide *agile* funding to fund MoD and the security needs of the country on a timescale that is appropriate to agile defence and security. This cannot be on an annual basis. A rolling ten-year defence budget, as promised by the Conservatives at the last election but not implemented, still would not allow MoD sufficient flexibility. MoD must be able to spend money when it needs to do so; but it will only save money when it can be reassured that the money saved will be available when needed. Because MoD has to cope with an inappropriate financing system, there is an obsession with buying equipment at all costs; so people convince themselves that the equipment is essential. This way of thinking is never challenged because no independent view is allowed. None of the recent conflicts has been accompanied by a reconstitution and regeneration programme designed to change the force structure towards that required post-conflict. The opportunity has been taken to reduce the size of the arsenal and/or the number of personnel. The most obvious example is, perhaps, the Royal Navy. But it applies equally to the other services.

2.3.3. The national scientific, technical and industrial base: regenerating lost acquisition capability and capacity

In the last three decades we have reduced our national R&D[6] capacity too, and we now allocate too little investment to R&D in our current acquisition programmes.[7] This has the perverse effect of increasing cost, time and technical risk in those programmes. This has been reflected recently in so many very costly and embarrassing defence acquisition failures that the point does not need labouring.

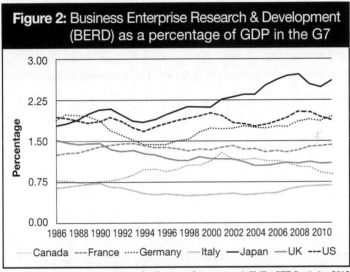

Source: Department for Business Innovation & Skills, SET Statistics 2013

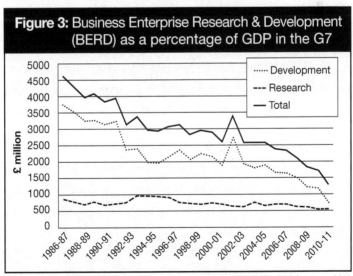

Source: Department for Business Innovation & Skills, SET Statistics 2013

Furthermore, if we cannot design or synthesise equipment, we cannot make it. R&D is the crucial factor. Throughout history, no military force that has sought to develop its own weapons has been able to do so without a vibrant research programme. Methods have changed, but the necessity for research, experimentation and prototyping has not.

The national defence R&D resource used to be vested in Defence Evaluation and Research Agency (DERA). The decision to split DERA into the Defence Science and Technology Laboratory (Dstl) and QinetiQ, which was privatised, was intended to increase the defence science and technology (S&T) base. This it failed to do, and arguably has had the opposite effect. Dstl now operates as an internal technical consultancy[8] with a small research budget to sustain the advice function. The large military presence that was a feature of the DERA was also dramatically reduced to make Dstl more competitive as a 'company', with no thought to the value their presence created to Dstl and to MoD more generally.

QinetiQ was floated to extract value from under-exploited technology and has been very successful, but it does not have the incentive to invest in new and speculative ideas as DERA did in the past, nor to remain focused on defence-relevant research. If a national capability or capacity is privatised and the new company owner cannot make money out of it, then the nation loses that capability and capacity, as has happened on a large scale over the past decade.[9] Much of the MoD extramural research budget is now spent in academe, but the large number of foreign PhDs and post-doctoral scholars that this supports means that less knowledge is retained in the UK than the funding could generate. This may not matter in civilian research with globalised companies, few of which have a UK intellectual hub, but it affects defence. It may now be time to revisit the decision on the benefits of intramural research, and to consider merging Dstl and the Centre for Defence Enterprise with the Defence Academy.

The UK's ability to produce inventions and innovations was a major factor in sustaining the close defence and security relationship with the USA. The UK had something the US needed and prized. Now that we no longer have the R&D capacity to produce many inventions, the mutual interest underpinning this relationship has dissipated, and the 'special relationship' is commensurately diminished.

It was always acknowledged that the military R&D produced major spin-offs to benefit the country. However, it was widely claimed during the Cold War that too much of the UK's national intellectual capacity was tied up in defence. But when the defence investment was reduced and military R&D was lost, intellectual development and innovation did not obviously migrate to other sectors. No compensatory civil R&D programme was established to serve the industrial base and no extra investment was made in universities to this end. The innovation capacity seems to have been lost. To be sure, there was a growth in *financial* engineering, but that has not proved an unalloyed benefit.

If the above Cold War argument was wrong, this is a most important point to note. It means that reducing defence R&D has been bad for the economy. The uniquely beneficial effect was because defence was a *national* programme, not driven solely by profit but by the commitment and enthusiasm of the participants, motivated to do something they believed in. This expresses the *value* of defence, rather than the *cost*. Another lesson that can be drawn from this is that privatisation and introducing business attitudes and procedures may not be the best way of improving defence. Research benefits spread across many applications. Studies by the US Office of Naval Research[10] suggest that basic research generates the highest returns, but these are not necessarily realised or attributed to the funder.

The intramural research programme also provided training for the cadre of staff needed to operate the acquisition programme. The absence of any alternative source of training was largely responsible for the decision to adopt a project management model that does not need the staff to have any domain-knowledge in the projects they manage. If the acquisition system is to be effective, a means for providing staff who have both domain and project management knowledge is required.

Some 90 per cent of the overall costs of any project are determined in the first ten per cent of the life-cycle. Those making these early decisions need the domain knowledge to understand the implications of their decisions on the life-cycle costs and projective life-cycle cost models to assist in their decision-making. Getting the research and development right, therefore, is crucial to realising value. Established best practice indicates that, across a portfolio of technical acquisition programmes, some ten per cent of the cost should be allocated to research and 35 per cent to development in order to contain the system technical risks and ensure delivery timescales. Arguably, the smaller the budget, and hence production run, the larger should be the percentage allocated to R&D to ensure the minimum of problems with the equipment.

It must be recalled that there are long time constants associated with both research and development. New science has historically taken some 40 years to be validated and disseminated across the technical community. Development may take up to 15 years depending on the novelty of the engineering involved. In complex weapon systems, a wide portfolio of research and development must have been completed to reduce project risk to acceptable levels. New means are required to help acquisition staff in MoD and the supply community acquire world knowledge more quickly and exploit it for R&D. This is part of the competitive advantage we seek.

It is difficult to obtain consistent data across countries defence programmes, but US Department of Defense (DoD) published data suggests that, in FY2013, the US Research:Development:Production ratio was about 7 per cent:34 per cent:60 per cent (assuming R:D:P volumes of $bn12:57:100). The UK figures are a little more difficult to interpret, but DASA's figures suggest that in 2011-2012 comparable UK figures may be 7 per cent:10 per cent:83 per cent (assuming R:D:P volumes of £0.55bn:£0.8bn:£6.8bn.[11] It is unclear how the £6.3bn spent on support is attributed). MoD senior management should ensure that the changes in these ratios and the reasons for them are understood, since they affect the volume, balance and health of our acquisition capability. If these are the correct MoD figures, then it suggests that MoD is either injecting risk into future programmes; not developing new equipment; or intending to abrogate all responsibility for risk and R&D. This needs clarification.

2.4 Acquisition processes

2.4.1 The fundamental principles of an acquisition process

Systems identification

Acquisition processes are necessarily creative, rather than procedural. They must be enacted by empowered, skilled, motivated staff.

Through 'systems identification' the acquisition community must first decide what is the nature of the systems to be acquired for a campaign, what interactions it will have with other systems (including those likely to be acquired) and with the environment within which it is intended to operate. Systems typically involve both equipment and services and are intrinsically 'socio-technical' in nature.

There are two classes of systems, each requiring a very different acquisition strategy:

(i) **Engineering systems.** These have a limited use for a given purpose, e.g. a rifle, boots. They constitute a 'static requirement', i.e. their use is unlikely to change over the life-cycle[12] of the equipment. They can be complicated or simple in design. With static requirements it is essential to avoid 'requirement creep' if costs are to be contained. Changing the requirement or increasing the specification half-way through the acquisition process can be very costly. So is artificially extending the time frame of the design and production process. There is normally a (frequently unspoken) requirement to minimise support costs so as to increase the effectiveness of the force.

(ii) **Natural systems.** These describe equipment which will come to be used for purposes other than originally foreseen. People will learn by using them, so the system needs the capacity to evolve. Acquisition of such 'dynamic' systems is complex rather than complicated, i.e. it is impossible to predict or describe how their use will change over their life-cycle, only to foresee that it is likely to do so. Software is an obvious candidate for approaching as a *natural system* requiring an *evolutionary approach*. Most military systems are natural systems by intent to make them applicable in the widest range of concepts of operation.

Evolutionary acquisition

The key to initiating a successful acquisition process is to make the correct systems identification from the outset, as the two systems require a fundamentally different acquisition strategy that incurs different timescales, cost profiles and possibly total costs, over the life cycle. An evolutionary approach can be used on engineering systems, but an engineering approach cannot be used on natural systems. To do so, to break them down into small simple components with set specifications ('reductionism'), is to guarantee failure. The NHS IT project is a good recent example of such a failure. The disastrous Nimrod MPA project would have benefitted from an evolutionary acquisition strategy.

The distinction between engineering and natural systems is crucial. In wartime, equipment such as tanks, missiles, etc. can safely be treated as engineering systems. But the longer a platform or system is expected to stay in service, the more it becomes appropriate to treat it as a natural system.

The US DoD insist on an 'evolutionary acquisition' approach for all identified *natural systems*, i.e. they buy a few items or the initial elements of the product, use it, learn from its features or performance, then develop it further, rather than trying (and failing) to specify all details from the outset. The US Defence Acquisition University insists on 'evolutionary acquisition' for all software. As real evolution is not linear, but it jumps and has extinctions, this approach ensures that failure will have only a limited effect. Projects that show no promise can be killed off before they become a ruinous waste of money.

MoD had great success with evolutionary acquisition in the torpedo programmes of the 1980s.[13] They demonstrated that they could reduce the life-cycle cost and delivery time of the complex software embedded in the torpedoes by about 50 per cent, and enable it to evolve as measure-countermeasure competition developed.

The importance of research and development

So far, we have addressed acquisition as it relates to equipment. But when we seek to acquire a capability there are other factors to consider. The most important of these are people and R&D, and the two are intimately connected. As we noted above, the inadequacy of our investment in R&D injects an enormous amount of risk into the acquisition process.

The reduction in R&D is not just for the physical sciences and engineering. It also includes the 'social sciences' including political and philosophical research, particularly research to understand the cultures of those with whom or amongst whom we compete and might have to fight. There is no research programme on governance and statecraft that could advise on the campaigns that we have engaged in for the last 25 years, which have primarily involved failures of governance in the places we have deployed to. Closing down research 'to protect the front line from cuts' removes experienced people and essential expertise from the system. This seriously weakens the front line. To turn a piece of equipment or service into a useable capability needs a community of people: to design, make, use, evaluate and amend the equipment, and to assess the circumstances in which it could or should be used.

ARMY 2020 (the British Army's response to the 2010 SDSR) recognises diplomacy, development aid, training and education as essential new 'weapons' to prevent conflict or advance UK's interests. Acquisition plays a part in acquiring (recruiting, educating, motivating) the *people* element of a capability as well as the hardware and software. How can we reverse the increasingly rapid and strategically important loss of talent? How will MoD's reform plans contribute to solving this problem, or will they make the situation worse? If privatisation of parts of the acquisition process is proposed, what should we have learned from previous experience? Did the split of DERA into Dstl and QinetiQ increase or decrease the intellectual and technical strength of MoD? Why did the government have to abandon GOGO?

COTS, MOTS, GOTS & Bespoke

The Organisation for Economic Co-operation and Development (OECD) 'Frascati' manual defines everything in the acquisition cycle to enable countries to standardise their statistics. MoD converted to these definitions in 1990.

COTS: commercial off-the-shelf
MOTS: modified off-the-shelf

GOTS: government off-the-shelf

Bespoke: the only alternative when the above are inadequate

Applying the normal rules of competition in the field of defence acquisition makes no sense when we are looking for something to give us a comparative advantage in the theatre of campaigns and operations. A comparative advantage can be achieved by both modification and *ab initio* design. A reduced budget means that we need to choose more carefully what equipment we try to adapt or invent. We will need to be able to reduce the proportion of our equipment which is specially made and concentrate more on what we can buy when we need it, adapting this for the required purpose. This is actually what we have always done in major wars when we adapt civilian equipment to the current military requirements. The application of this principle is most obvious in the Royal Navy, which can benefit most dramatically from this cost-effective wartime procedure in today's time of rapid change.

In addition, at a time of rapid change such as today, it is important to invest more in weapons rather than in platforms. Modularised weapons can be retro-fitted cheaply to a variety of platforms. There are a few notable exceptions to this rule and, in the current situation, there are some weapons systems for which it still makes sense to organise their acquisition and replacement over long periods; the nuclear deterrent would be one. But for the rest, maintaining an irreducible minimum core of weapons and equipment and designing a fast, efficient system to acquire what else we need when we need it (and to dispose of it profitably as soon as its utility is past) would appear to be a sensible option. An ideal ratio of 90 per cent COTS or GOTS, nine per cent MOTS, one per cent totally new might be a target to aim for.

Along with systems identification, *customer status* is the most sensitive issue in the acquisition saga. This is where we need very good people who are technically competent to make the decisions. This cannot be done by generalist or non-specialist managers.

2.4.2 Managing Acquisition

Acquisition is a *socio-technical*, not simply a *technical*, process. Because it involves the complex interaction of people and equipment, it requires a good knowledge of systems engineering by all involved. *Project management* is but a small part of acquisition, rather than the dominant role that is now allotted to it in MoD. This is challenging, for the majority of acquisition projects are now controlled by managers who do not have technical expertise. It is a very serious mistake to assume that they only require a 'business knowledge' to enable them to manage any business or government enterprise. This marginalises the technically competent and suppresses the sources of innovation, i.e. researchers and users, upon whom effective defence acquisition depends.

The changes in the UK economy have not been mirrored in the changes to MoD management of acquisition. The decline of manufacturing as a proportion of the GDP of the UK, including the defence industrial base, poses a major challenge to improving equipment acquisition, not least because there are far fewer technically competent people available for defence to draw on. The situation may be more encouraging for services, as the economy has switched to emphasise services. This provides one reason for the need to change the balance in the forms of power we employ to advance our interests. Managing services is radically different from managing equipment, and MoD should recognise this.

The civil servants in MoD have been deskilled primarily by a narrow understanding of performance management and a failure to recognise and reward technical or professional expertise in defence and security.[14] The senior civil service (SCS) in particular continues to insist that there is no need for domain competence: *any* SCS member can run MoD with no previous experience – as witnessed by recent senior appointments. If MoD cannot recover its position as a technically literate intelligent (and expert) client, it will not acquire the right services and equipment when needed and will therefore not provide value to the taxpayer. Furthermore, in time, such a customer also destroys the *supplier's* competitiveness. We cannot sustain a viable security industrial and commercial base without a technically literate client and owner. Even the non-executive directors in MoD do not appear to have been chosen for their military, technical or political excellence in security. The Chief Scientific Advisor does not appear to be a Board member now, either.

MoD has persistently changed its provisioning organisation and processes in response to evident failures, frequently identified both by the National Audit Office (NAO) and by parliamentary select committees. In general, the changes implemented have been proposed by external management consultants, and some have been implemented by them too. However, as judged by further cycles of criticism by NAO and parliament, none of these solutions has resulted in an organisation that is fit-for-purpose and capable of evolving to meet changing needs.

MoD requires a range of acquisition processes appropriate to the systems to be acquired. New 'one-size-fits-all' approaches have not worked and will never work. The failure of this investment in management consultants in an attempt to solve MoD's acquisition disasters demonstrates the need for a range of processes specifically tailored to the needs of MoD, evolved by those accountable, including those politically accountable.

MoD's acquisition management methods must similarly reflect the needs of acquisition, not the desire of the senior civil service for conformity with performance management. Acquisition requires strategic management across the whole security community, management that involves the community, motivates them through their participation and welcomes their creativity. Lives depend on it.

The reduction in our acquisition budget will require new forms of partnership involving government, industry, commerce and academe to generate the systems needed. The acquisition budget will need to change to multi-year, dynamic financing to reflect the uncertainty in the campaigns that we must be ready to undertake.

2.4.3 The disadvantages of defence prime contractors

Defence prime contractors were once an important idea because of their ability to integrate the many components needed for complicated weapons and platforms, and to bring these into mass production on a scale appropriate to mass industrial warfare. As the fall in demand for weapons and equipment began to bite after the end of the Cold War, the UK attempted to create large defence entities to compete with US counterparts, seeing size as the key competitive advantage. This strategy has failed.

Previous MoD improvements have sought to achieve the impossible by removing risk from the owner or customer and passing it to the supplier at no penalty in cost, performance, responsiveness, inventiveness or quality. This encouraged the supply industry to pursue the route to monopoly and to form very large international corporations with no national, and sometimes unknown, allegiance.

The argument for large-scale defence prime contractors ('defence primes'), which have become monopolies, was to simplify the relationship between the public customer and the pseudo-private supplier. It was also claimed it would reduce and remove risk by transferring it to the defence prime. It may have removed the political risk, but it has not removed the technical and financial risk. Technical and financial risk cannot be shed. In defence, risk is in the end owned by the customer, not the supplier. Not only do cost overruns tend to come back to the taxpayer (because otherwise the project becomes unviable) but the wrong or badly made weapon will cost the life of the soldier, sailor or airman, not of the manufacturer, civil servant or minister.

The current problem with primes was accelerated in the mid-1990s when the MoD offloaded onto the private sector its responsibility, as 'owner', to bear the risk of equipment development. This was at a time when defence companies were already under great stress from rapid political and technological change. Offloading production could be justified. Offloading risk could not.

Whitehall was beguiled into believing that defence markets were like civilian markets. They are not. Defence markets are always closed, run by political considerations rather than purely commercial ones, and wise nations never sell their best kit. As a result of MoD's policy, many smaller companies went out of business.

Many in the big corporations are exasperated by dealing with MoD but they have no incentive to change the current system. They have adapted to the bureaucratic model. They can use their retired military to manage their relationship with MoD and keep their best technical people to handle rich foreign customers who retain technical expertise. There are also no incentives for MoD civil servants to change the system. It protects them from risk. Moreover, there is no personal incentive to reduce costs.

To recap, the concept of relying solely on defence primes is obsolete because they are not adapted to the small volumes of equipment we are now acquiring and our need to acquire more services. Defence primes are needed for only a few complicated systems. For the rest they are a massive unnecessary cost. Similarly, large framework contractors and Private Finance Initiative (PFI) contracts have done much to waste money and destroy flexibility and innovation. All tend to destroy true competition. Making defence primes and framework contractors into large, virtual monopolies so as to be more internationally competitive has had the unintended consequence of suppressing innovation in UK industry. Reducing competition and innovation further increases the cost of acquisition. The defence primes' supply chain is just as problematic as MoD's. Primes, even in the USA, are now facing problems in that they are not getting the diversity of ideas they need to cope with the speed of change in the international security sphere.

The alternative for the UK government is directly to support, exploit and develop the SME industrial base. SMEs tend to be innovative, low cost and effective. They lose these advantages when forced to work with large companies. Government departments and the civil service have lost the skill of working with SMEs and the prevalent culture continues to make it increasingly difficult for them, rhetoric to the contrary notwithstanding. MoD, the Department for International Development (DfID), the Ministry of Justice (MoJ) and the Home Office are all alike in this. This has become a major concern for government acquisition. The Cabinet Office is rightly trying to rediscover how to work with SME's in the IT sector because they are much more innovative, and operate on a relatively tiny cost base.

Since we must move quickly towards an adaptive military model, we need networks of companies that can produce quickly and in relatively small quantities what is needed for a campaign. We should be developing small companies' networks, exploiting this British national trait as our competitive advantage. Using this network of small companies will stimulate our intellectual capability and grow the economy in a way that subsidising the defence primes' monopoly will never do. In order to use small companies, MoD will have to make a lot of adjustments to its working practices. For example, although small companies can overall be a lot cheaper, profit margins need to reflect volume. Big companies with huge, long-term orders can manage on the notional seven per cent. Small companies with small contracts need at least 20 per cent. The UK Trade & Investment (UKTI) Defence and Security Organisation (DSO) would be part of such networks to restore our competitive stance in exports. The problem with finance is illustrated by the BIS/industry establishment of the Aerospace Growth Partnership (AGP). This is aimed at regenerating the UK aerospace sector. The UK aerospace sector has some 17 per cent of the fixed-wing world market by revenue, estimated variously to be in excess of $3,200bn over the next 15 years, or some $213bn p.a. This equates to some $36bn p.a. to UK aerospace. If the R:D:P ratio were to be 10:30:60, say, and there was a 20 per cent profit margin, then UK aerospace should be investing some $290m p.a. in research and $87bn p.a. in development on average.

This should be a self-financing business model. But apparently it is not. The AGP has so far invested some £300m at Cranfield University – in essence recreating DERA's aerospace research and development activities. This may be partly due to the financial sector's reluctance to fund R&D for activities in the timescale beyond five years, and partly to address the research that was not undertaken since the late 1990s, when MoD dismantled DERA and BAE Systems (Britain's largest defence company) withdrew from new aircraft programmes, closing its Sowerby Research Centre.

Recreating the cumulative investment in infrastructure and intellect will take some time, and considerably larger investment than the £300m spent thus far. Not least will be the provision of some of the world's fastest supercomputers and experimental facilities to validate the new software required. It is to be hoped that a sensible investment programme can be assembled to re-establish the concept of the National Aeronautical

Establishment that was originally intended for Cranfield and RAE Bedford: a partnership between government, industry and academe. This must include acquisition in its research portfolio.

The new idea of a 'National Arsenal'

BAE Systems has never been a truly independent private company because there is no such thing in defence.[15] Nor is there a 'natural market' for defence and security equipment. What we have is simply a variant on the traditional concept of an 'arsenal', using the same funding methods, but with different management methods. Today, in BAE, we have not so much a large defence company but a state-created monopoly, an ineffective national arsenal. The question we have to address is, how are we going to transform our national arsenal?

If we decide *not* to do so, we must then identify how we *are* going to provide adequate weapons systems and services for the armed forces[16] we are going to need. If our forces are going to have superiority of weapons systems and services for the forms of power we elect to employ across a campaign (as opposed to performance of weapon vs. weapon in an engagement), how will we provide it without a national arsenal? We cannot compensate for inferior weapons with people: we have too few people and cannot afford casualties.

If we are going to maintain a national arsenal, then we need to find a different model of arsenal. Given the size of our defence budget, of our R&D and of our defence industry in our post-industrial economy, the only arsenal which makes sense is one based on a larger slice of our general national economy, i.e. to create our military and security capability and capacity from a prototyping civilian-based economy, designing and making weapons based on civilian processes. To do this effectively, we need to understand what the UK as a whole today is capable of generating. This does not mean just by our defence industry but by our civilian industry, by the City, on the basis of our education system, through the abilities of our indigenous population, ethnic communities etc.

This still needs government long-term funding. Private companies have research time scales of nought to five years to comply with demands for return on commercial funding. All BAE's new projects originated in government-funded, long-term research. But this stopped in 2000 when DERA was split. At that point, the BAE prime contractor model failed. Moreover, by then the volume of work had fallen below the point of critical mass.

The evolution of MoD

We must never forget that the real customer for the acquisition process is not DE&S, but those who will have to wage the campaigns of the future, i.e. the armed forces. For acquisition to enable and sustain the new strategic concept for acquisition which we are now developing, there needs to be an intimate, interactive relationship between the two. But the current system separates acquisition from its real customer: the armed forces. The most recent proposals will separate them even further. The MoD system is intent on installing a fixed, unadaptable programme regulated not by the services' operational needs but by rigid, budgetary-driven project management.

It comes to many as no surprise that the Chief of Defence Materiel, Bernard Gray, should complain that he was worried and frustrated by the failure of his efforts to 'fix the programme'. The basic assumptions on which everything in the current acquisition system is based are flawed at a fundamental level. The fixed programme that MoD proposes to install is now of questionable relevance and the notion of a 'fixed programme' ignores the fundamental challenge of defence policy, which can never be fixed, but must always be flexible and agile. The fixed programme suggests that the MoD is reduced to no more than a contract delivery department, which is a denial of what defence should be about. The fact that defence policy in the 2010 SDSR was not even determined by MoD but in the National Security Council (NSC) underlines how divorced MoD has become from its true purpose.

Is what MoD is doing to reform itself going to fit it to develop and run an acquisition process appropriate to a defence budget of two per cent of GDP? From the evidence available, the answer would appear to be a resounding *no*.

There has been no strategic assessment of whether the overall management process was the best one or not for the country's defence and security establishment. This urgently needs to be addressed because, firstly, the current performance management method – with its stress on individual advancement rather than on the collective performance which we usually associate with national safety – is more than ever philosophically unsuited to today's challenges in Whitehall.

Secondly, it is this management process which has contributed to the technical deskilling of MoD. The leadership of MoD has now installed a management method that does not itself depend upon technical expertise or domain competence. The Chief Scientific Advisor, who used to sit on the Defence Board with the same rank as Permanent Under-Secretary of State (PUS) and Chief of the Defence Staff (CDS), has been removed from the Board and downgraded in rank. Only two military people now sit on that Board. The technical and domain competencies of the other Board members compare most unfavourably with those of past years.

As a direct result of this trend in managerial methods in recent years, our acquisition system is no longer sensitive to socio-technical or military performance. The acquisition process is in the hands of generalists, as if there were nothing technical about war. The emphasis of the programme management is now not on performance or military utility but on cost and time, and civil servants will be blamed or rewarded accordingly. This system can only calculate *cost*, not *value* – value can only be determined by measuring what is acquired against what we need when we need it. All this is demoralising and is a strong incentive for the competent to leave MoD, especially to leave the acquisition system, and seek employment elsewhere. We can sympathise with the Chief of Defence Materiel, Bernard Gray, in his sincere efforts to halt the haemorrhaging of talent; but without challenging some fundamental features and values of the present system, the task is hopeless.

The final irony of MoD's management system is its total lack of adaptability, the very quality we now recognise we need above all in our future armed forces. Just as armies have to be able to evolve in contact with the enemy if they are to win, so management has to evolve to deal with new challenges if the organisation is to survive. Constructive, sensible change cannot be driven by people, insiders or outsiders, who do not understand the business of defence and security. We would not expect our commander in Afghanistan to turn to big consulting firms for advice on the deployment of his troops. Why should they be considered so qualified to propose how MoD should be run? Moreover, a system that is driven by efficiency criteria that take no account of the need for the staff to continue their education, to enable them to identify the adaptations MoD requires, is doomed to fail. MoD must become a self-adaptive organisation, stimulating changes before they are critical. This apparent increase in investment should be more than compensated for by the improved value.

3

Creating a Healthy Culture for Acquisition

3.1 Acquisition culture

In developing this paper, it became clear that the complexity of acquisition makes it difficult to find solutions sufficiently simple to be politically advocated or for non-specialists to understand easily. We have chosen to use the term 'culture' as a way of explaining the complex network of interacting influences, outlined below, which in no small measure determine whether or not it will be possible to establish an effective acquisition system. Acquisition *culture* is taken to mean the grand strategy shared by the security community, which includes the acquisition community.

In order to make the culture tractable and explain our approach, we have clustered the influences into three sets. But this is not to suggest that the sets are independent; they are all closely intertwined, *viz:*

Philosophy: the philosophy underpinning our grand strategy depends on our assessment of the instabilities (conflicts, problems, natural disasters etc.) that we have or expect to face; on the values that underpin our interests; on the campaigning we undertake, with its associated complexity, networks, and the need for agility;

and on the impact of our current smallness, the available arsenals, the abilities of the security community.

Practice: the delivery of grand strategy depends on intelligence, research, education, and training; and on the fitness of governance, the role and competence of parliament, the appropriateness of funding mechanisms; and the capabilities and capacity we invest in.

Self-adaptation: ensures that our acquisition can evolve to become and remain fit-for-purpose and, in its turn, help the security community to learn to adapt, stimulating change by investing in education and by recognising the community, challenging them rather than berating them.

3.2 Philosophy

3.2.1 The security environment of the early twenty-first century

Today's security environment is dominated by the rapid growth in world population (up by a factor of four in the last 60 years and not yet slowing) and the increased competition that this generates; and by the increase in communication within the world through ease of physical and electronic communication and the increased co-operation and diffusion of knowledge this stimulates. In the main, the UK seeks to influence the remaining 99 per cent of the world population in ways that are mutually beneficial.

Among the effects generated by the above factors is the weakening of the nation state as the unit of competition, and the growth of power of the 'network state'. Nation states may be home to several network states, not all of which have the host country as their primary identity. Other non-state actors also contribute to the complexity and instability of the security environment. We face increased opportunities and threats from more capable competitors & collaborators, demanding that we too build competitive capacity and actively manage our alliances (e.g. the Commonwealth, EU, NATO). The underlying nature of today's security environment we have termed hypercompetition. Hypercompetition is a form of permanent campaigning, and this has a profound impact on acquisition. Successful acquisition increases deterrence and improves the value of alliances.

3.2.2 Security as investment

The instabilities that may arise in this highly interdependent world require that we develop the capacity to generate a wide range of forms of power and to employ them coherently in campaigns that advance UK interests. These forms of power require appropriate, agile, adaptable forms of acquisition for the services and systems involved, plus appropriate governance and competent organisations.

Acquiring these forms of power should be viewed as an investment that is employed daily in providing security rather than, as it has been to date, an insurance to be drawn on spasmodically: hypercompetition needs a new funding model that reflects this change. It includes economic warfare. This requires reconsideration of Crown immunity and the meaning of law, and poses the questions: can 'international law' displace 'national law'? And whose 'law' will govern acquisition with international suppliers?

3.2.3 Security budget determined by investment value

The volume, balance and health of our investment in security should be judged by a set of measures related to 'values'. This cannot happen without knowledge of how to determine values, and without changes to our governance that recognise this difference. Similarly, the campaigns we select to engage in should be subject to a value analysis prior to our participation.

The Defence Economic Advisor must become the Security Value Advisor, with a suitable staff and an active research programme. The NAO will need to develop new methods to assess the value of acquisition, not just the cost-effectiveness, and to judge the health of acquisition, the appropriateness of the balance and the volume and rate of investment.

3.2.4 Security to be financed by a 'bank'

As discussed above, financing campaigns that include hypercompetition requires multi-year investment, agility and adaptability. Existential threats require the construction and maintenance of viable deterrents that are permanently deployed.

Private Finance Initiatives are an inappropriate solution with a long term impact. Existing PFIs should be renegotiated, given the current low interest rates.

3.2.5 Campaign-based arsenals

Whilst we constrain the defence budget to two per cent of GDP and fail to exploit related security budgets, we should recognise that this constrains the power we can employ to counter threats to the UK and to exploit opportunities to advance our interests. The 'bank' should develop a reserve to fund campaigns short of existential wars. This builds on the concept of contingency funds managed by the Treasury to include 'normal' funding.

The long campaigns we have engaged in over the last 25 years have consumed our 'arsenal' with little or no hope of reconstitution, since it was created at budget levels of four per cent of GDP and higher. The forward programmes should be formed with this in mind.

Since the envisaged levels of investment in security are too small to permit the recreation of a complete arsenal, an arsenal will have to be procured for any significant campaign we choose to mount. This places huge demands on intelligence and acquisition.

The portfolio of power we must wield changes the nature of what we mean by the term *arsenal*. It is no longer likely to be dominated by 'kinetic weapons' manned by increasingly fewer people but, unless the scale or concurrency demands a large 'force', it will include many highly skilled and educated people competent in a wide range of activities not previously considered as military. Private security companies have re-emerged in recent campaigns as significant parts of our security capacity. Planning for expansion must include them too.

Many of the equipment products and services will have value across several of the campaigns we need to undertake, particularly if designed using modularity and commonality, where this does not impose penalties and warrants similar unit costs. These common products and services should form part of the *core acquisition programme*, along with the long lead-time equipments needed for nuclear deterrence. Additional equipments and services may need to be included in this new 'arsenal', developed to the prototype stage, where infrequent acquisitions mean that we need to retain design teams and to refine the manufacturing techniques and plant needed for rapid acquisition. The core is there to expand to meet the needs of campaigns, and contract when the campaign is over, at which point reconstitution/regeneration/replacement are required: we cannot fight old wars better, new wars will be different.

3.2.6 The security community

We have concluded that the approach to acquisition must change across the whole security community. The first requirement is for a recognition that such a community exists de facto and that this must be made *de jure*.

Binding this community requires organisational and cultural changes, beginning with a shared understanding of grand strategy and the need for a competitive stance to guide planning. This community must also be capable of self-adaptation. The people tasked with leading and implementing this process must engage in active learning to appreciate this evolution. External expertise can help here but cannot replace the need for this community.

3.2.7 Synthetic environments

Synthetic environments-based *procurement* (SEBP) rather than *acquisition* (SEBA), in the sense in which the terms are used in this paper, is a relatively mature concept. But SEBP has so far failed to extend its scope to include the strategic and policy communities fully to make it into SEBA by linking grand strategy to the creation and realisation of operational concepts. This is largely due to the failure to educate those in the strategy, policy and political leadership roles in how to use SEBA to advance UK interests.

Synthetic environments provide the framework to support the partnership required between the stakeholders in agile capability development (parliament, government, industry, academe and commerce), as well as to address the functional issues. The ability to prototype and experiment rapidly with novel forms of power demands a close partnership between the policy, financial, scientific, engineering, making, supporting and using communities, with appropriate arrangements to protect the intellectual property rights (IPR) of the partners and stimulate innovation. The MoD has components of this already, but needs to formalise and expand the concept into a coherent basis for an agile future force. If the Defence Academy could be merged with Dstl and CDE and returned to academic status, it would facilitate the establishment of an *Agile Capability Development Centre* with a network of universities, civil and defence industrial suppliers. The US is pursuing a transition of this sort by establishing its Rapid Fielding Directorate under the Under Secretary of Defense for Acquisition, Technology, and Logistics (USD(AT&L)). Other countries, notably France, Netherlands and Australia, are evolving down similar paths and have long operated a close partnership between government, academe and industry.

The security community will be required to create and deliver a wide range of powers. It will need to be composed of personnel on a wide range of contracts, from permanent Crown Service to occasional retained contractors. As campaigns are undertaken and require more, and then fewer, personnel, we require the ability to increase and reduce the acquisition staff correspondingly. This needs an education and training capacity to support this variation. New means of supporting commercial enterprises to contribute to the security community are required, based on investments rather than subsidies.

3.3 The practice cluster

3.3.1 Open-source intelligence in the era of 'big data'.

One feature of the networked world is the availability of information and data about the world from internet based sources – the era of 'big data'. We need a radically different understanding of the use of open-source intelligence, providing the context for detailed intelligence. This changes the balance of importance between open and closed source intelligence. We will not merely process more of the readily available data, but develop means to abstract and filter the data to help people understand what is happening.

Used intelligently, we should be able to improve our modelling and understanding of the threats and opportunities we face, whether intervention will advance our interests and what form of campaign and arsenal we would need to mount the campaign.

However, it also directly impacts on acquisition by making clear what we may be able to acquire directly, what we can modify, and what we must counter asymmetrically. Commercially, we can exploit the 'competitive intelligence' used in commerce to better advantage, especially in identifying potential supplier networks.

3.3.2 Knowledge and information

In order to provide the community with the capacity to evolve in response to changes in the UK, the wider environment, and in the behaviour of our competitors and collaborators, we must undertake research into new models of governance and statecraft, in addition to our traditional technological research programmes.

Research must be increased considerably. One way to do so without an increase in budget would be to merge the Defence Academy and Dstl, and link them better with academic and industrial partners. Research also needs to be linked to experimental formations from all the services and to other organisations that generate the many forms of power we now need.

An in-depth, objective analysis needs to be made of the consequences of accepting a large number of overseas students to do scientific/technical research in the UK, perhaps effectively denying the places to UK students or educating our competitors. This is delicate issue, but it needs to be addressed as knowledge is a key issue in hypercompetition. How do we evaluate the competing interests and the relative value to UK interests of the income these students generate compared to the advantage their education brings to a country which may not wish us well?

Cyber security is a well understood topic within MoD and in some parts of academe, commerce and industry. But it is not well understood elsewhere. The coupling between civilian and security communities through their use of the common internet, particularly in acquisition, poses many challenges if we move to SMEs as suppliers. Government will need to provide advice and a secure infrastructure as necessary.

Information and influence are key aspects of hypercompetition and are therefore now things we must consider as subjects for acquisition. Their importance as elements of any campaign today is evident to all. However, our traditional strength in this area has been much diminished in recent years; the UK has reduced its investment in the BBC World Service, BBC Monitoring, the British Council and in Commonwealth programmes.

Hypercompetition involves many other forms of power used as weapons. This includes, for example, the financial weapon, in addition to the wider economic weapon. Given London's claimed pre-eminence in this field, acquisition for future conflict means we need to explore how to develop and use offensively this form of power, as well as reducing our vulnerability to attack. The same applies to the other forms of power in which the UK is strong, however awkward it might be to address these issues.

3.3.3 Acquisition practice

The prevailing climate of 'risk avoidance' in both parliament and government is one of the most pernicious aspects of the current acquisition culture; both now try to hide from the issues of ownership of acquisition. Doing so by establishing one or a few large suppliers may help to finesse problems with the finance and delivery of the equipment programme and provide a source of blame, but it will ultimately destroy the flexibility and capacity for innovation that an adaptable acquisition system needs. The innovation found in UK SMEs, particularly in companies around 200 employees in size, suggests that this is where our real strength in these qualities lies. MoD/BIS will accordingly need to reconsider defence industrial policy.

All acquisition needs to understand the operational concepts affected by the equipment and services to be acquired; the life-cycle of the equipment and services; the market for them; and the cost and socio-technical issues involved. This can only happen within a community committed to satisfying the needs of the services and of the country, not driven by the need to maximise revenues for shareholders. This needs a radically different, more flexible approach to contracts, particularly with SMEs, affecting profit margins and IPR.

3.3.4 Changes in governance

One of the essays below in this volume addresses the changes in governance of defence and security in the UK which have occurred in recent years, and which in no small measure have contributed to the problems MoD and our acquisition system face today.

To these must be added the potential for a major constitutional change, with increased federalism likely to appear. This will impact further on the governance of security, and the responsibility for acquisition may be more difficult to coordinate. However, we suggest that the principles outlined in this paper are robust to whatever form of constitutional settlement is adopted.

A concept to explore in further studies might be for parliament to assume greater ownership of security on behalf of the people, leaving government charged with managing it on behalf of parliament. The US Congressional model is worthy of our scrutiny here, to note its advantages and disadvantages. There are major implications for the role of civil servants and private security contractors (PSCs) working in the security sector. For example, means will need to be found to accredit PSCs and ensure that they are fully able to integrate with UK forces when required, and appropriate, adaptable forms of acquiring their services will need to be developed.

To address the issue in greater detail of how to move to better forms of governance for security is beyond the scope of this study, but it is a crucial element in creating a healthy culture for acquisition.

3.4 Self-adaptation: acquisition is about people

In essence, the security community must be able to adapt constantly if it is to retain fitness in a changing world, and to help shape that world to advance UK interests. Furthermore, it needs the capacity to acquire not only classic weapons, but also all the systems and services that enable the range of powers needed to campaign effectively. This cannot happen by importing external agencies (defence companies, consultants) to run the system; it requires the creation of a healthy national community organised and managed participatively, espousing the nation's values and committed to pursuit of the national interest.

3.4.1 Evolutionary development

Creating a healthy culture for acquisition will require a long term approach. Implementing changes involves a significant bottom-up as well as top-down re-education programme and will take many years. Some personnel will not wish to change, and ways to redeploy their talents must be found to retain morale among those who wish to stay.

Supporting Essays

The Strategic Environment

Rear Admiral Chris Parry

Introduction

Our acquisition process needs to be able to identify and incorporate the context within which human, technological and material resources need to be applied to achieve political and societal aspirations and ambitions. This context enables priorities to be established and both human skills and technological solutions developed to meet future requirement, rather than producing legacy systems and platforms that are obsolete by the time that they enter service. Despite the inherent risks of attempting to map the future in detail, a coherent view of the future operating environment and the likely trends also allows a reasoned judgement to be made about the scale of flexibility and technology insertion that needs to be factored into all procurement programming and design. In addition, it enables a shared vision and understanding with major platform and system suppliers that transfers some of the procurement risk – and exorbitant adjustment costs.

The next ten to fifteen years will witness a fundamental shift in the balance of economic and military power across the world and in various discrete regions. This trend will have a substantial effect on where the UK perceives its interests to lie and the ways in which it provides for its economic health and security. However, while much is changing, it is likely that the overall geo-strategic advantage of the developed world will persist, with only regional and technological adjustments to the overall correlation of military power. Nevertheless, the UK will need to remain agile and alert in strategic terms if it is to align itself in relation to these subtle yet transformative changes in the international landscape.

The turbulent teens

The geo-political landscape will be one in which democracies coexist with a range of 'managed' democracies, authoritarian regimes and outright autocracies, some with opportunist and expansionist tendencies. At the same time, global economic activity, having lost the ideological edge provided by the conflict between Marxism and capitalism, will be defined by intense competition between different forms of capitalism, ranging from the free market philosophy of most liberal democracies and their partners to the variously controlled state and regime-led versions evident in many emerging and aspiring states, including, notably, the 'market-Leninism' of China.

As such, the second decade of the twenty-first century is likely to be characterized by the uneven, complex interplay of differing political and economic systems. Further competition is likely to arise between those regional powers that seek to limit the international system for their own ends and those states whose prosperity and security depend on the maintenance of an open system of trade and access. This competition will be particularly marked at sea, where various states will seek to extend their jurisdictions further out into the oceans, in order to provide strategic depth and to exert control over marine resources and the means of access.

Amid the rivalry between states to maintain political and economic advantage and to exploit access to global markets, there will be an unstable balance of competition and cooperation between states and within states, which will periodically flare up into confrontation and occasionally conflict. In some countries (both democratic and authoritarian), internal tensions will revolve around the gaining or retaining of political legitimacy, through the struggle to maintain social cohesion, ensure economic survival, improve the lives of populations or to maintain elites and regimes in power. Traditional groupings and alliances will continuously be tested in relation to this dynamic environment, with states making decisions in relation to the risks and opportunities as they present themselves, in the interests of maintaining geo-political influence, in ensuring the stability of their societies and in sustaining economic growth. In these circumstances, individual states and commercial concerns are likely to have multiple identities and allegiances, as well as national interests and pressures which will militate against and conflict with their obligations to established partnerships and alliances.

States will therefore compete at some levels of interaction and cooperate at others; in future, they are likely to espouse a shifting pattern of alliances and security arrangements reflecting the range and diversity of risks that they need to confront. A philosophy reminiscent of Lord Palmerston is likely to prevail: 'We have no eternal allies and no perpetual enemies - our interests are eternal and those interests it is our duty to follow.'[1]

This trend is evident in the way in which China and Russia (for the moment) align in those geopolitical areas that enable them to compete strategically with the US, and cooperate with each other, both economically and institutionally, when it suits them. As part of an obliquely expressed determination by both countries to 'de-Americanise' international institutions and those parts of the world considered vital to Russia (the hinterland of Eastern Europe, the Baltic Sea, the Black Sea and the Arctic) and China (the Western Pacific and the sea and land routes to its energy sources, raw materials and markets) it is clear that Russia is seeking to limit and exclude US influence in and around Europe, while China seeks dominance in east and South-East Asia. Russia's promotion of the Eurasian Economic Union and China's construction and development of both land and maritime silk roads through Central Asia and across the Indian Ocean respectively, together with China's proposed Asia-Pacific Free Trade Agreement, demonstrate that the competition with the US is not just military and geo-strategic but also commercial. There is the distinct prospect of the bulk of Eurasia being dominated by the understanding and cooperation between China and Russia. With increasing Chinese commercial and energy links with the Gulf and a long-established relationship with Iran, it is likely that the bilateral Russian-Chinese relationship will be expanded to include Iran and, by extension, other Shia populations.

These trends suggest that both Russia and China have gained as much as they consider possible in an open, globalised world and together are seeking to establish alternative trading and security arrangements that will maximise their advantages in relation to the US, Europe and other powers. Both countries have already expressed their dissatisfaction with international rules and arrangements about which, they have claimed, they had little influence at the time of their agreement. The establishment of the Asian and BRICS Development Banks (in opposition to the World Bank, the IMF and the dominance of the dollar), together with infringements of the international law of the sea (UNCLOS) – by China – and various missile and nuclear agreements, as well as the invasion and destabilisation of sovereign states (Georgia and Ukraine) – by Russia – are indications that this dissatisfaction is not mere rhetoric, but a concerted policy.

Overall, the geo-strategic pattern emerging appears to denote a strategic and economic competition between a Eurasian axis dominated by the partnership between Russia and China and the democratic, free-market states of the Americas and elsewhere. This places Europe, the US, Canada, India, Australia, Japan and South Korea in an informal ('maritime') relationship with each other, one which will be confused by their conflicted commercial and strategic discrete interests in their relationship with Russia and China. The Trans-Atlantic and Trans-Pacific Partnership proposals by the US (which currently exclude Russia and China) will intensify commercial and economic rivalry between the two blocs, while the relationship will evolve within, and reflect, the context of increasing military modernisation and investment by not only China and Russia, but also by several so-called non-aligned countries.

Within this pattern, future strategic and economic competition is likely to concentrate on access to:

- commodities (food, water and raw materials)
- energy sources (oil and gas, but, increasingly, renewable installations and the security of distribution networks, grids and storage)
- markets outside the newly aligned Eurasian and maritime 'blocs'

- the Polar regions and their resources
- habitable and arable land
- the cyber and electro-magnetic environments
- space
- the sea (especially through exploitation of the resources of the high seas and deep oceans) and oceanic trade routes

The progressive reductions in developed countries' military spending and the accompanying rise in that of aspiring powers is also changing strategic assumptions, the balance of risk and opportunity and the practical utility and moral obligations associated with traditional partnerships. During the next five to ten years, without significant changes in attitude in developed countries, a fundamental shift will take place in the way in which political and military power is distributed and applied, both across the world and even within Europe. Within Europe, countries are increasingly unwilling or unable to commit their armed forces and the US is becoming cynical about European will and capabilities. As we have seen, the rise of regional powers with wider global and military aspirations, such as China, Russia, India and Brazil, and a host of complex transnational issues and transformative shifts in the world's economic patterns are already fundamentally altering the strategic balance of the early twenty-first century world. These factors and trends have altered US perceptions about where its interests lie and where its emphasis needs to be placed, most recently demonstrated in the US's pivot (back) to the Asia-pacific region. More importantly, both China and Russia are developing armed forces which by the early 2020s will be able to compete in their regions with US forces in quantitative and qualitative terms and be able to threaten and use both nuclear and conventional capabilities in support of their wider diplomacy, economic interests and political objectives. In particular, area denial and anti-access platforms and systems will make the risks of going in harm's way and defeating sophisticated missile and other offensive systems prohibitively costly, both in terms of casualties and in relation to the cost ratio between defensive and offensive systems. However, it can reasonably be expected that technological solutions and the alteration of the geometry of the battlefield through novel applications, such as unmanned systems and stealth, will present opportunities to overcome these difficulties in time, coupled with new military ways of achieving political objectives. In all cases, there will be renewed military emphasis on the use – or denial of use – of the sea, space, cyber-space and the electro-magnetic spectrum.

Elsewhere, the strategic landscape will be characterised by the pressures and strains of a world population heading for 10 billion people by 2050, of which 70 per cent will be urbanised and a fair number living in mega-cities of 24 – 30 million, whose governance and sustainability will present challenges and opportunities in equal measure. This aspect will introduce a fundamental change in the way in which states and cities are managed and the relationship between the two develops, together with new forms of social organisation and control. In addition, the effects of climate change, in terms of changes in land use, sea level rises and migration will have an unsettling impact on established states and communities, exacerbated by pervasive inequalities and imbalances in global and regional levels of access to all forms of human security, opportunity and resources.

Two regions are particularly vulnerable to these pressures. They will play out most severely in the

Middle East and North Africa, where demographic imbalances, lack of economic opportunity and the pre-modern conflict between Sunni and Shia Muslims will continue to cause instability, terrorism and violence, both in the region and in the wider world. Indeed, the conflict between the two branches of Islam will determine the character of most political and social issues in the region for some time to come, indicating a sustained period of both proxy (as in Iraq and Syria) and direct confrontation and conflict between states and communities, which only an accord between Iran and Saudi Arabia seems likely to moderate. Demographic, climate, sectarian and other divisive transnational trends are also likely to affect the regions of South and East Asia centred on the Bay of Bengal. Not only is the region framed by the potential strategic and commercial rivalry between India and China, as well as a struggle for influence and market access in South-East Asia, but also the interests of outside powers in strategic and economic terms. There will also be the struggle by regimes of whatever type to maintain their hold on power and claims to legitimacy.

Further causes of instability at local and regional levels will include ambition, ideology, greed, ethnic animosity, residual territorial claims, religious fanaticism and competition for resources (especially agricultural land, mineral wealth, water rights and oceanic resources). Refugee flows, a desire for socio-economic improvement and population migration driven by conflict, economic and environmental collapse or natural disaster will generate demands for international assistance and, additionally, spawn terrorist actions, communal violence and ethnic disturbance, further exacerbating relations between states. Comprehensive approaches, collaborative mechanisms and the will to engage in the long term in the common interest, involving all forms of political, economic and technological power, will be required to deal with these complex and interrelated issues.

These trends and historical experience suggest that the period until 2025 is likely to witness the rise of regional confidence-building, mechanisms to deal with transnational problems and security arrangements (similar to NATO) in the face of specific regional or external threats, the containment of animosities and disputes and dealing with a series of overlapping risks. Beyond NATO, this trend is already apparent in South and East Asia, in South America, in the Gulf and is increasingly possible among the broader Arab community of nations. There is of course a possibility that these regional arrangements could lead to the establishment of confrontational blocs, with the distinct chance that in the complex modern world they could find themselves in competition with each other at some levels (diplomatic and military) and cooperating at others (economic and cultural).

The United States

Much has been written in strategic commentaries about the shift from a US-dominated unipolar world to a looser multi-polar arrangement. Economic stagnation, fiscal pressures and the experience of extensive deployments to Iraq and Afghanistan have made the US wary and weary of foreign military intervention. With recent conflicts demonstrating the limitations of the utility of its military instrument of power in situations short of conventional war, at which it remains pre-eminent, the US will be more constrained and more nuanced in the use of its military power. With the rise of China's military capability and the modernisation of Russia's capabilities by 2023, coupled with other powerful regional capabilities around the world, the US will be less able and willing to intervene in all regions of the world. Indeed, it is probable that the US will expect its regional allies and partners to contribute a lot more in containing and dealing with regional threats and risks, while providing back-stop cover and grudging intervention if its partners and allies get out of their depth.

This is because, despite its formidable military capabilities, US commitment to overseas ventures and activities that do not directly support its vital interests will become increasingly discretionary and subject to more constrained political will and a reduced domestic appetite to bail out what are considered feckless and free-loading partners. As such, global security will be determined by the extent to which the US considers its economic and strategic interests to be identified with, and best served by, globalisation, an open trading system and cooperative international institutions. The result is that US hegemony and its reactions to crises will be expressed by a series of balance of power calculations about various regions of the world, with powers and groupings asserting themselves either in collaboration with the US or in opposition to it.

However, despite recent economic shifts and strategic distractions, the US is still the world's sole economic and military hyper-power and is likely to remain so, if by a slightly smaller margin in relative terms. As a result of its renewed confidence and the exploitation of unconventional oil and gas reserves, which will make it energy independent by 2035, it will, by 2020, be a reviving political and moral force, with an economy strengthened by new industrial and re-shored enterprises, a favourable demographic profile and steadily rising growth.

Therefore, as the world's most powerful democracy and probably the most vibrant per capita economy, the US will remain the indispensable partner for the UK and many other allies and partners in undertaking military operations at high intensity, in those activities that require advanced technological applications and in deployments that need to be sustained over time. It will be active in countering challenges to regions vital to US interests and those areas vulnerable to strategic competitors and maintaining access to the global commons, notably the sea and space, cyber-space and the electro-magnetic spectrum. This approach is likely to be accompanied by the adoption of a more sophisticated, agile approach to expeditionary operations, one that is characterized by speed, precision, integration and low footprint/high impact operations. This will rely on strategic enablers, principally air and sea platforms that can deliver highly networked, mobile, low footprint force packages of task-based and task-configured manpower and munitions, whose sustainment will be supported by a mosaic of partnerships, prepositioned facilities and forward deployed bases, both by land and sea.

This suggests that the US will adopt a more discriminatory approach to the use of its military instrument of power, coupled with more sophisticated use of its moral, cultural and diplomatic tools at its disposal. It will seek to conceal its strength and rely more on 'force withheld' as an instrument of strategic-military policy. It will expect its regional allies and partners to play their part and pay their way in credible, tangible and not just totemic ways, while keeping its powder dry for those occasions when deterrence has failed and its vital interests are threatened.

NATO

The North Atlantic Treaty Organisation (NATO) has been the most successful and operationally enabled political-military alliance and collective security organization in history. In the post-Cold War environment, it struggled to define its purpose amid perceptions that the military threat to Europe had receded and, through a series of strategic and domestic political evasions, enabled and encouraged the drawing down of European capabilities even as its geographic ambition expanded. Since then, it has been subject to differences in approach and emphasis between its North American and European elements and marked asymmetries in military and funding capabilities between its members, exacerbated by a serious economic recession starting in 2008 and leading to a prolonged period of low growth and financial volatility. The EU is similarly constrained by declining defence provision and the definite prospect of economic stagnation, although individual countries, such as the UK, Germany and the Scandinavian members have established the basis for sustaining economic growth.

However, given the commercial rivalry that has emerged with China and Russia, the fact that European countries have been infiltrated economically by investments and joint ventures by these two countries, especially in terms of infrastructure development, property ownership and energy provision, makes coherent, unified responses to strategic challenges difficult. This aspect was particularly relevant in relation to sanctions applied to Russia in the wake of its invasion and destabilisation of Georgia in 2010 and of Ukraine in 2014.

Despite the fact that not all NATO missions in recent years have attracted general support from its members, with Germany and Turkey in particular proving reluctant to compromise their national agendas, it would appear that there is universal support for NATO as an institution. Especially in view of Russia's recent actions, it seems certain that the US and its NATO partners will continue to support unequivocally the overriding commitment to collective defence of the Alliance's territorial integrity and freedom from attack, as enshrined in Article 5 of the Washington Treaty as the bedrock of the Alliance. However, the political rhetoric will in future need to be backed up by appropriate readiness profiles and actionable capabilities, other than the threat of nuclear release, if the Alliance is not only to deter and defeat threats to its territorial integrity, but also to resist coercion and bullying at individual and collective levels, especially by a Russia committed to its dissolution. Above all, it needs to have the political will to put its forces in harm's way when its members' core principles and values are at stake.

However, the Alliance also needs to do more to secure its borders and societies from non-military threats, notably in relation to destabilising influences by other states, criminal and terrorist groups, trafficking and illicit migration. A new NATO strategy needs to concentrate on the security of its members in a comprehensive way, taking into account all risks and threats that threaten its human and territorial security. This necessarily has to consider the proliferation of – and changes in the philosophy of use of – nuclear and other weapons of mass effect.

For the time being, it seems likely that the US, while turning towards the Asia-Pacific and other regions, will continue to provide at least the potential of nuclear and missile defence guarantees for Europe, along with a commitment to reinforce its allies should an immediate, overwhelming (military) threat emerge. The emerging strategic dilemma for the US is whether the NATO Alliance should remain central to US strategy in the unfolding twenty-first century or be viewed as a cluster of declining regional states, with which the US may have recourse to act or depend on from time to time. In response to crises in and around Europe, when it assesses that its own vital interests are at stake or its strategic partners are threatened with immediate, overwhelming conventional or nuclear force, the US is likely to adopt a strategy of graduated response and progressive escalation, reinforced by the implicit threat in extremis to use nuclear weapons. This means that, except in these circumstances or if Israel is threatened, the US is unlikely to want to continue to station large numbers of forces abroad, including in Europe.

Implications for developed countries

Increasing technological sophistication, reduced resource provision and the drive for improved efficiency and effectiveness in developed nations have encouraged the exploitation and integration of joint assets and co-operative solutions in response to crises requiring military forces. However, as in the US, for the next decade or so, the political will and public appetite in developed states for conducting unilateral intervention operations and state-building under arms will diminish, meaning that major enduring commitments which do not involve vital interests are unlikely to occur. The age of national discretionary interventions, except in a multinational construct and with United Nations sanction, is drawing to a close. Increasingly, states are likely to resort to the use of collective solutions (when available) and proxy actors – sub-state actors and client states (and possibly private military companies) – to influence the will, decisions and attitudes of actual or potential opponents and competitors.

These collective solutions will be required to respond to a widening range of contingencies arising from the need to contain a range of crises and risks. These will include the need to counter state-based opportunism and adventurism in areas of strategic importance, countering proliferation of weapons of mass effect and disruption, countering irregular activity (especially extreme criminality, proxy violence, arms trafficking and terrorism) and dealing with collapsing and failing human space, including humanitarian and disaster relief operations.

Armed forces will also be required to assist with the consequences of migration, ensuring access to natural resources and bolstering the international system. In offsetting critical demographic imbalances, the UK and other developed nations will look for technological solutions, unmanned systems and increased use of private service companies in all activities that do not require immediate battlefield access or uniformed personnel.

At the same time, crisis management will have become more subtle and dynamic, with some, notably developed, nations' governments preferring to use non-military levers to deal with the causes of problems whilst retaining military options to deal with the more threatening symptoms. Enhanced co-ordination and co-operation will be required between nations, governmental departments and NGOs involved in crisis management (along the lines of the 'Comprehensive Approach') to ensure the most successful, discriminating use and timing of military force or influence.

Of course, the context within which crises take place and the consequences for various states will determine the structure and the national composition of the forces that are likely to be made available to deal with them. Informal and impermanent groupings and spontaneous communities of interest are likely to emerge in response to specific threats, as with the recent surge in piracy off Somalia.

Equipment

The coming decade will see the entry into operational service of new weapon systems across all environments, primarily associated with increased precision and greater lethality that only require smaller forces to deliver them, using unmanned/robotic systems. In addition, directed energy, nanotechnology, electromagnetic weapons and increasing numbers of space-based sensors and systems will become more widely available and at lower cost.

The next decade could also possibly see the return of low-yield nuclear weapons that are considered by some states to be usable in war on land and at sea, as a key component of some states' war-fighting – as opposed to deterrence – postures. This approach is already explicit with regard to North Korea, Russia and China, and is occasionally implied by India, Pakistan and Israel as well. It is possible that a more explicit policy and range of flexible responses might be readopted by NATO or the US, both in order to offset demographic, resource and conventional force imbalances and to deter the threat or use of nuclear weapons.

Meanwhile, developing nations will seek to offset the advantages offered by developed nations' armed forces through investment in sea and area denial and anti-access systems, while China and Russia will adopt more advanced regional and, later, global, power projection platforms and systems. Other developing countries' military power is expected to increase in step with their economic growth, global interests and political aspirations. This will be particularly true of India, Brazil and Japan, but may extend to all those developing countries that have sovereign issues to dispute or resources to protect, both by land and sea. However, some weaker nations may chose the sensible asymmetric response of using a range of different forms of power, rather than just military.

The interconnectivity, commercial penetration and open access associated with globalisation, together with the determined efforts of some states to acquire intellectual property and technological advantage through illicit means or espionage, will result in the narrowing of the technological advantage enjoyed by the US, its allies and its partners. Alongside the expanding trade in trafficked, counterfeit and copied systems, these trends also mean that sophisticated weapons and systems are likely to be acquired by non-state entities and groups, especially proxies, terrorists, criminals and separatists. More importantly, larger populations and especially those in mega-cities are dependent on mobile communication, networked infrastructure and computerised systems for their prosperity survival. These dependencies and technologies have a completely different set of vulnerabilities, from physical, cyber and electro-magnetic points of view, which both state and non-state actors will exploit.

The United Kingdom

In this complex strategic environment, the survival of the UK as a sovereign entity, its prosperity and its health as a democratic society depends critically on territorial integrity, the preservation of the rule of law, freedom from coercion and on the ability to conduct vigorous economic and institutional activity in an economically globalised, but politically and geo-strategically fractured environment. Although the UK's position is now geographically more remote than any other European country from likely sources of direct threat, the UK remains a globally networked state with respectable international influence, numerous vital interests overseas and critical investment in the maintenance of international stability and law. Here, the sea and air lanes of importance to the United Kingdom largely coincide with those vital to NATO as a whole and Europe in particular. Indeed, the interdependence of the global economy and the reliance of the developed nations on a stable and secure international environment will make it impossible for the UK to ignore transnational problems and threats to the global commons (such as the sea and space), the symptoms of which are increasingly likely to be addressed in ad hoc arrangements – or coalitions of the willing and able – sometimes under UN mandate, but more often composed merely of interested parties, who may or may not be familiar with each other.

For now, the UK retains significant and substantial political, commercial and diplomatic advantage in maintaining a close relationship with the US and Europe. However, the perception of its utility to the US cannot be assumed or taken for granted; without the ability to exert influence or project power in support of, or in parallel with, US interests and priorities, the UK will have little leverage over the US or to call on its assistance in case of need. As a result, its military partnerships will need to revolve around membership of NATO, with parallel structures that seek to develop an identifiable and credible European capability for concerted action, more particularly in the face of coercion and regional crises. These partnerships will exist alongside and overlie bilateral relationships and regional agreements that best serve more distinctively British interests in the wider world.

Within the next five to ten years, it is likely that traditional mechanisms and security arrangements will prove unable to deal with the scale and diversity of emerging crises associated with a more assertive Eurasian bloc, the regional powers, the realignment of states as they seek to position themselves in an increasingly resource-constrained and competitive world and amid a range of difficult transnational issues. In parallel, it is anticipated that the UK's European partners will seek to enjoy the benefits, but avoid the burdens of collective security arrangements, with attempts to role-specialize and burden-share defence functions, to the detriment of overall security. They will attempt to reduce costs by engaging in increasingly collaborative, but progressively declining capability in both relative (to threats and risks) and absolute terms. Meanwhile, the US will no longer necessarily be prepared to be the force of last resort enabling Europe to resist coercion and direct action. It will concentrate on supporting and cooperating with those geographic areas and partners that best secure its vital interests.

As such, for the near future, it seems likely that the UK will require its armed forces to remain roughly congruent with (and useful to) the US, have the capacity to provide lead or framework status, commonality and capacity within Europe (or as part of an ad hoc coalition) and retain a stand-alone national capability to protect vital national interests such as the Falklands. To offset and deter coercion by states deploying mass conventional and nuclear capabilities, the requirement for a credible national strategic deterrent will remain, but will need to take into account new assumptions about nuclear coercion, threats and use, as well as more diverse emerging technologies of mass effect in the post-post-Cold War strategic environment.

In order to maintain influence and a capacity for intervention world-wide, it seems likely that Britain's future military capabilities and relationships will be selected by virtue of their ability to contribute to the achievement of Britain's vital interests, wherever they might be found. This trend suggests that Britain will seek to be more strategically agile and adaptive and to maintain military partnerships where mutual interests can be identified and for just as long as those interests remain. It also means that future relationships and groupings that reinforce and secure British interests in a globalised political and economic environment are likely to be found and developed among new and more diverse partners and within several overlapping security institutions, while preserving the collective assurances provided by a reinforced and refreshed NATO in its traditional collective defence and security posture.

Categorising the Threats and Opportunities

David McOwat

For most of the twentieth century, the UK faced a straightforward, relatively limited range of 'instabilities' (i.e. threats to the stability or survival of the social, economic or political system we were striving to uphold), dominated throughout the period by a clear threat to our national existence from one quarter or another. The range of responses to these threats/instabilities shaped our national institutions and our national attitudes. This legacy we still live with. It is particularly evident in (but by no means restricted to) our military system. The deadly serious nature of these existential threats and, for much of the period, the importance of maintaining the Empire, meant that the UK was prepared to spend a high proportion of its national wealth on military forces, seeing them as the principal means of countering threats and advancing the nation's interests.

Today, and as far as we can foresee, the direct, clearly evident existential threat is somewhat diminished. We maintain a nuclear deterrent and a (much-reduced) conventional deterrent to counter this threat as we perceive it. But today we also face a wider range of other types of instability which we need to be able to deal with too. Individually, none of them may appear to be as serious as the twentieth century threats from Nazi Germany or the Soviet Union were, but they are serious nonetheless. Indeed the very fact that they are not so obvious, and in many cases not best countered by classic military means, makes it harder for the public and politicians alike to understand the collective dangers (and sometimes opportunities) which these instabilities present. As a consequence, there is a reluctance to invest in the means necessary to counter (or exploit) them.

So that we can determine how best to provide the UK with the appropriate, effective tools to deal with the unpredictable future, it is helpful to categorise the kinds of instability we face or are likely to face. There are several ways to do this. The following suggested classification is based on the underlying reasons for, rather than the physical manifestations of, the problem. The argument for choosing a classification based on this principle is that it should help us to focus on the causes, rather than on the symptoms, of the problem. This should give us a better chance to forestall or prevent a conflict (or aid recovery so as to prevent conditions being created that would cause future conflict) rather than just fight one.

In addition to the existential threat, we would identify at least four main categories of instability we need to prepare for. These are:

(a) **Colonial legacy.** Best exemplified by the 1982 Falklands conflict, this would involve the UK in a classic military and diplomatic struggle on a limited scale against a reasonably modern enemy, probably in a distant part of the world.

(b) **Failure of governance.** Instability, manifested by conflict or upheaval, caused by a weakening or collapse of state competence resulting in a government's inability to cope with a serious problem. The Balkans and Afghanistan fall into this category. The 'Arab Spring' instabilities are an excellent, on-going example. By identifying and monitoring 'countries at risk of instability' we can go some way to foreseeing where this kind of instability is more likely to occur and, if we monitor the regions well, perhaps also when. Classic military force may have some utility in these cases, the most likely being to create a secure space so that other means can be deployed to stabilise the situation. But those 'other means' are the key to long-term success. An internal example of a failure of governance might include the failure of our education system which has produced an unemployable, disenfranchised 'underclass', or the failure to integrate ethnic communities and handle their different cultural and religious identities.

(c) **Natural or man-made disaster.** Humanitarian operations to cope with sudden natural catastrophes (e.g. tsunamis, hurricanes) or to forestall or prevent tragedies made (or made worse) by man (e.g. famines, floods of refugees, epidemics), are the classic stabilisation target. If the military are deployed here it is not usually for their fighting ability but because they are a powerful, disciplined force capable of operating in difficult and dangerous situations.

(d) **Hypercompetition.** This is the most prevalent and insidious form of instability in today's world. Conflict and competition are being waged by ever more varied and ever less predictable means. What constitutes a weapon in this new 'hot peace' no longer has to go bang. Energy, cash as bribes, corrupt business practices, cyber-attack, assassination, economic warfare, information and propaganda, terrorism, education, health, climate change or plain old-fashioned military intimidation are all being used as weapons of hypercompetition. Some national governments and sub-state groups have recognised this situation and have embraced this new form of conflict/competition, using it most effectively. Others, such as our own government, have not, despite the fact that the City is increasingly aware of hypercompetition, having to cope with it on a daily basis.

The Evolving Asymmetric Threat and the Irrelevance of Structures

Jonathan Shaw

The MoD's 'Future Character of Conflict'[1] study (FCOC) posits a future threat environment in which our opponents will evolve their threat in order to create the asymmetries required to evade our strengths and exploit our weaknesses. The challenge for defence is to create a force capable of coping with this evolving asymmetric threat.

Special Forces (SF) are often cited as the masters of asymmetric response. To the extent that this is true, there are many contributing factors, not least their ability to draw as they choose on capabilities that are held at readiness by other forces. But at the heart of the way SF do their business is an essential point that contributes directly to their asymmetric adaptability: they do not structure themselves permanently for operations, rather they task-organise for operations in pre-deployment training (PDT). The (semi-) permanent structures are human, the extra kit and skills are lashed on according to task. The premium is on intelligent, well educated, well trained individuals who can re-task and re-group at speed, and can take under command and absorb other assets and capabilities as required.

Adopting this approach to force-generation poses different problems to each service and particular problems to the army. The major RN and RAF equipments are defined by their technological possibilities and their flexibility is therefore limited. Both RN and RAF train *units of capability* (e.g. ships, aircraft) which are then packaged for task. For the army, the malleability of army formations/units and the range of separable skills make for a potential flexibility that is almost infinite.

The army bases itself on the *harmony*[2] assumption that it will need to deploy forces designed to endure, i.e. conduct operations continuously in a specific area. Consequently, any structure (e.g. brigade/unit) needs five copies to be sustainable; but what to put into each structure? As the range of potential enemies we might face, or the scope of each enemy's evolution over time, is limitless, so potentially might be the scope of competences required of these structures – replicated five times. This is clearly absurd; so a somewhat arbitrary decision has then to be made, on affordability or probabilistic grounds, of what to include in the brigade structure and what not to. Hence the proposals for the multi-role brigades (MRB) (based on the need to maintain five copies) with supporting assets (i.e. no longer contained in theatre troops).

The argument for these MRBs is that they make a best guess at providing for the range of capabilities from which the actual power required (kinetic or otherwise) can be generated as required. This solution minimises the turbulence of re-task-organising in pre-deployment training whilst maximising the benefits of personnel cohesion. The arguments against this solution are that MRBs are expensive and that they are inappropriate to the demands foreseen in FCOC.

- **Expense:** MRBs make wasteful investments precisely to provide the fat from which to draw the force actually required – replicated five times. Defence cannot afford to fund such profligacy.

- **Irrelevance:** MRBs are based on the flawed premise that the force required can be predicted and hence structured for in advance. Even if (and that's a big if) the MRB predicts the threat the enemy originally poses, by the logic of FCOC (and the evidence of Northern Ireland, Iraq and Afghanistan), a thinking, evolving enemy will alter the threat over time to exploit the 'flanks' exposed by our capabilities; so the later brigades will need to be altered accordingly. Indeed, the more a force has its capabilities hard wired for public display, the more an opponent can spot the flank and turn it ab initio (e.g. Chinese technology has already made our aircraft carriers currently being built irrelevant even before we can complete them).

The basis of future conflict is people. The army in particular needs to explore the option of basing its structures on manpower organisations to which the requisite equipment and skills are added at PDT, when the shape and actual requirements of the task have been devised. An initial, generically structured, trained and equipped 'fire-fighting force' will be needed, held at high readiness, to buy the time to identify the requirement and create a more appropriate force. This will involve the army in getting used to fighting wars with a constant stream of prototypes. Yet, in fact, this has been the experience in Northern Ireland, where the counter-IED and other electronics constantly evolved; in Iraq, where the kit always changed at a bewildering speed; and in Afghanistan, where no roulement has been configured like its predecessor.

By focusing on the human dimension of the army, this procedure – a large-scale version of what SF already does – would play to what FCOC says we will need to capitalise on: our people. It will, of course, require a more flexible and affordable acquisition system for equipment and services. That, in turn, will require our defence industry to gear up for rapid and evolving equipment orders, drawing, where possible, on civilian production, rather than embarking on huge, long-term (and hence, for today's campaigns, out-of-date) programmes of the sort that equipped us for World War II and the Cold War.

Acquisition and the Special Relationship

C. N. Donnelly

A key issue for UK interests and UK national security today is how to maintain the UK's 'special relationship' with the USA. On balance, this special relationship is of real importance to the UK, but also of some worth to the US. However, it is neither permanent nor guaranteed. We cannot take it for granted. It needs to be worked at constantly, refreshed and renewed. The US may well lose out if the relationship fails, but it will not notice the loss as much as the UK will.

Which special relationship?

There is a special relationship between the US and the UK based on a long history, a shared language and culture, and a fundamental mutual emotional attachment. However, it is the second aspect of the special relationship we are concerned with here, that is, the significant US/UK military/security/intelligence relationship which has existed since WWII. The two aspects of the relationship are interlinked, of course, but they are not the same thing, although they are often treated as if they were. The UK and US emerged from WWII with a high degree of mutual respect. But the US grew in strength whilst the UK withdrew from Empire and diminished in global importance. For this reason, the burden of sustaining the special relationship falls principally to the UK.

Unfortunately, this second aspect of the relationship appears to have been significantly diminished recently by several factors over and above the turning away from Europe by the US. These are: the UK's indifferent military performance in recent conflicts; the run-down of our intelligence capability; and the perception (on the part of the US and other allies) that the UK is no longer investing sufficiently in its military to be able to play the leading role it used to do in Europe, both as an operator and as a technical innovator.

From the US side, the relationship was driven not so much by emotion and history, but by how much the US needed something from the UK to help the US develop and maintain its superpower status, i.e. what the UK could provide to the US in this regard that the US could not itself produce. The UK, of course, wanted the security which US military power provided, and the intelligence to underpin our own position in the world. In other words, the relationship was always determined by a dominant theme of self-interest: the UK and the US needed each other, albeit for different reasons.

However, it is important to recognise that the special relationship has not been allowed to override US interests. For example, in the defence acquisition sphere, the US has always seen the UK as a rival. The special relationship did not prevent the US from acting against the UK when economic interest was at stake.

The two main pillars

What the UK has traditionally contributed to the US as the foundation of the 'Special Relationship' has been based on two main pillars:

Knowledge and experience, including intelligence-gathering and analysis; technical expertise, especially inventiveness, ideas and scientific information; the experience of having dealt with a situation new to the US

Political and military support, wherever this supported US policy interests and to help the US get what it wanted in the world

Being able to provide something the US wants and needs is still the only reliable way to get US respect and to maintain the special relationship. Today, this is translated into whatever will help the US to maintain its position in the world, promote US interests, contribute to stabilising the world and ensure US economic well-being. The original two pillars remain at the heart of the relationship, although they can be supplemented by other interests as time moves on. How these interests are expressed in practice is the essence of the problem facing today's UK government. If we can still provide something useful for the US, something they cannot do for themselves, then they will be prepared to reciprocate very generously. This is not a symmetrical exchange. Nor is it an issue of cost and payment. Rather it is a barter deal. If the US can buy what it is deficient in on the world market, then there is no basis for the special relationship.

Knowledge

The US needs to know what is going on in the world, and what is at the cutting edge of technology, if they are to maintain their status. President Obama has recently (December 2012) reiterated that the key to America's security is to maintain a generational technological advantage over all other nations (close allies included).

How do we ensure that the UK has some technology the US needs, and knows something that the US does not?

Only advanced research and high quality intelligence can provide this. In the past decade, culminating in the SDSR, we have run down our technical research and development capacity in many key areas to such a degree that our scientists and researchers can no longer engage with their US counterparts on an equal footing. The UK used to lead the world in research into, and understanding of, several crucial defence and security issues. We have now lost that position.

With less than two per cent of our defence budget spent on R&D, and following the destruction of DERA and with it much of the national R&D capability, we are generating very little technological invention. We have not so far harnessed our national commercial and academic research to fill this gap. Moreover, the government's higher education policy has led to universities selling their research skills. The US Defense Advanced Research Projects Agency (DARPA) funds research at UK universities, the results of which go back to the US, not to the UK.

Political and military

UK usefulness to the US could be direct and bilateral, or it could be through the UK's role in international organisations such as NATO, the EU and the UN. Declaratory political support (e.g. votes in the UN etc.) still has an intrinsic value. But the ability to deploy and employ hard power in support of US interests and policy is by far the most important asset. Here, the reduction in our military capabilities and capacity is having a real impact. Along with capability and capacity, we have also lost some of the outstanding reputation we used to hold in many of the other crucial military fields too, such as submarine operations.

Several factors have traditionally made the UK's deployment and employment of military power useful. They can be present singly or in combination:

(a) A willingness and ability to deploy a significant size of effective armed forces (i.e. well-trained, equipped and led) to reinforce a US main effort, including a readiness to share causalities

(b) The ability to employ other kinds of power to achieve an effect which supports US policy or interests. This could be economic power, political influence, a technical ability, such as cyber-warfare, or a civilian state-building or humanitarian relief capability.

(c) The provision of support in a field in which the US is weak or has inadequate capacity, or in which the UK is especially competent. Military examples might include naval mine-sweeping or army special forces.

A key question here is: how important to the relationship is it for the UK to have the capability to provide forces able to operate with US forces at little or no notice (a day-1 capability), and able to match the performance of their US counterparts? If the cost of acquiring and maintaining this capability in all our major systems is such that it severely reduces our capacity, this policy assumption has severely impacted on our acquisition policy and should be reviewed. Particularly in a field where the US is already well-endowed (e.g. aircraft carriers, fast jets), such day-1 support might be much less valuable to the US than an ability to provide greater, more sustainable support at 30 days' notice, or support in a domain of expertise or in an area of the world where the US is not strong. This has serious implications for our acquisition.

A brief look at other allies with which the US has some sort of special relationship casts light on some of the above considerations. For example, the US values very highly the advanced research and inventiveness which Israel produces. Israel currently commits over 20 per cent of its defence spending to R&D. The UK used to spend on average 10 to 12 per cent, but, as we noted above, this has now fallen to under two per cent of defence spending, and at that level we are just not credible players in the field. The 'research' component in the Research:Development: Procurement ratio is well below that needed to sustain competitive capabilities. The US has a very high regard for the radical conceptual thinking which the Australian Armed Forces have recently produced in response to the demands of modern conflict. This conceptual work is seen by the US as well in advance of that being done in the UK, despite the smaller scale of the Australian defence effort.

As noted above, if the intellectual product which the US so highly valued from the UK could be purchased freely on an open market, then there would be no basis for a special relationship. This would be a client relationship. Some allied states actually want a client relationship with the US, finding a sense of security in that arrangement. But the UK's special relationship has always been based on peer-level engagement and respect in the specific technical, military and political areas on which the relationship is founded. If the UK loses the ability to provide its contribution from a position of self-reliance and intellectual equality, a serious problem arises.

For example, if the UK simply provides troops for the US to command without an independent, competent command capability, or if the UK commits to acquiring US-built aircraft, but cannot persuade the US to release the computer codes which will allow the UK to develop the aircraft independently, then the UK is in a subservient role, with no freedom to deploy independently – and the special relationship is changed fundamentally as a consequence. To maintain the special relationship requires that the UK have the political and professional competence to act as a critical friend and offer a loyal challenge to a US plan or policy when it appears misguided, or when it would be contrary to UK interests. No one better expressed this principle underlying the special relationship than Dwight D. Eisenhower: 'Only strength can cooperate. Weakness can only beg.'

Sustaining and restoring the special relationship

Although the special relationship has in the past been sustained by specific features, and it seems that these are still very valid, it is likely that, in addition to these traditional things, there will be new issues where the UK may be able to provide something the US needs.

Research and development is perhaps the most obviously relevant factor for our acquisition policy. This would involve sponsoring and pursuing advanced research (with experimentation and practical engagement in the problem area) into issues relevant to current and future conflict, this regaining the UK's reputation for the best thinking in defence and security. The global recession demands radical new methods for preventing, engaging in and recovering from conflict which are appropriate to the complex challenges we will face for the foreseeable future. This presents an opportunity to re-establish our reputation, provided we increase the budget devoted to creating ideas and organise ourselves so that we can actually do so. Without reinvesting in creativity we will not be able to guide an advanced research programme because we will fail to stimulate new conceptual ideas.

Developing the capability of UK instruments of power would be the second field to explore. This would involve identifying radical and innovative ways for the UK to enhance its national instruments of power, especially armed forces and intelligence services relevant to current needs, institutions of diplomacy and statecraft, and instruments of state-building and other non-military tasks relevant to current conflicts and international competition. This would ensure that, despite budgetary restraints, the UK can continue to provide a meaningful contribution to global security as valued by the US.

It is important, with reference to the above, to appreciate that 'research' and 'development' are interactive. Developing a piece of equipment, a concept, a tool of social engineering is in itself part of the research process. When the problem is rapidly changing, then it is R&D agencies which also produce the greatest effect. Acquiring a capability and adequate capacity in cyber-warfare is another current example. It is the researchers and developers of cyber-capability who are the best and most advanced practitioners of this art. Once there is an attempt to institutionalise a new and rapidly-developing capability, innovation and experimentation will be killed, development will stagnate and the sought-after capability will quickly become obsolete – out-dated by the competition. Capabilities which are sensitive to the 'measure-counter-measure' process should be implemented by a research organisation, not by a 'production organisation'.

Conclusion

If we continue on our current path, the UK will soon have lost the special relationship (and Europe will have lost a crucial bridge to the US). Reinvigorating the relationship depends on regaining our strength and our reputation in the fields of intellectual and technical excellence, and for being able to provide meaningful hard power or other relevant support to the US where and when it is most needed. It also requires us to develop better mechanisms to influence the US than we currently have.

Again, Eisenhower expressed most succinctly this current challenge which now faces us all: 'Our real problem, then,' he said, 'is not strength today; it is rather the vital necessity of action today to ensure our strength tomorrow.'[1]

The Operationalisation of Defence Industries: The Critical Military Component

John Louth

Introduction

Over the years, the science and art of military operations and force projection have generated an in-depth, though contested, body of knowledge, derived from both the practitioner and academic. This has been drawn from the depths of antiquity, with Sun Tzu's conceptualisation of political and military strategies,[1] through to books and emerging reviews on lessons and consequences of our recent wars in Iraq and Afghanistan. Understanding the role and significance of commercial businesses working in the defence and security markets to a nation state's military component and the corresponding potential for state violence, legitimate or otherwise, has populated a much smaller, niche genre.

This is far from ideal, for what we are left to contemplate is a historiography moving at two distinct speeds – one fast, the other slow. Whereas our understanding of notions such as geopolitics and the use of military operations seems ever more sophisticated (though not always ever more insightful), our grasp of the purposefulness of defence industries to the national defence and security effort has progressed very little. The aim of this essay is to hint at the need for a subtle process of intellectual and practical realignment.

My colleague and fellow author Trevor Taylor refers to the story of defence in the United Kingdom since the end of the Cold War as residing in three distinct dimensions: defence policy (direction and review); defence management (initiatives and failures); and military operations.[2] Paul Cornish and Andrew Dorman write of a four-cornered defence model involving policy and ideas; military ability and strength; financial resources and national industrial; and economic capacity.[3] Both approaches are highly useful and competent, though seem to concede that the conceptualisation of defence businesses as a critical component of a state's power and ability to assert its will through the projection of military capabilities remains woefully neglected.

This paper considers the modes and methods of interaction between government and industry that are necessary to generate defence capabilities. Thereafter, the economic imperatives of defence and security industries are discussed, with BAE Systems used briefly as a fractal of the larger market. The paper then goes on to assess the skills and competencies to be found within the industry base, suggesting that these intangible assets should be conceptualised as critical components of the national economy. To begin, though, a short diversion, by way of a story, on a subtle, visible difference between the first Gulf War in 1991 and the operation in Afghanistan in the early years of this century.

Iraq to Afghanistan: a simple comparison

Jacques Derrida is a very difficult contemporary thinker to understand properly.[4] His core philosophical idea seems to be that meaning can never be completely grasped within a text or story as key words and phrases provide pathways to the truth of a subject that a complete treatise or text cannot articulate. This simple yet, paradoxically, sophisticated notion may help with the themes of this essay.

The political and military analysis of the first Gulf War in 1991, when a US-led, United Nations endorsed, Western and Arabian alliance attacked southern Iraq to liberate Kuwait from its Iraqi occupiers, is fairly comprehensive.[5] Within this ever-expanding body of work, the activities of the Royal Air Force's Tornado ground attack force is extensively covered. The broader conflict of 1991 was characterised by pervasive media coverage with images of air attacks and exploding laser-guided ordnance, a nightly occurrence on British television screens during January and February 1991. The Tornado was at the epicentre of the British contribution to this air campaign, with the force drawn principally from the RAF Bruggen wing of IX, 14, 17(F) and 31 squadrons. Interestingly, and significantly, the maintenance, engineering and logistics front-line support for the Tornado force in theatre (beyond embedded squadron engineering staff) came from 431 Maintenance Unit, also based at RAF Bruggen in Germany. This independent unit comprised engineering and logistics specialists who contributed significantly to keeping aircrew and aircraft flying during a very intensive air campaign. It was comprised almost exclusively of specialist RAF personnel, supplemented by some specialist from the British army. Civilian contractor involvement from commercial businesses, in 1991, was statistically irrelevant.[6]

Let us now roll-forward to Britain's involvement in operations in Afghanistan a decade or so later. The situation relating to direct defence industrial participation in operations has changed dramatically. In July 2008, 22 companies employing over 2,000 people were holding contracts with the MoD to provide direct engineering and logistics support to British troops on operations in that country. By 2010, at the height of the British in-theatre effort, this had grown to some 67 companies employing 4,867 civilian personnel; an increase of specialists on the ground of some 240 per cent from two years earlier. By 2010, within Afghanistan, contractors formed 35 percent of the deployed military manpower from the United Kingdom. This represented more than 45 per cent of the total UK overseas military effort when measured by input costs.[7] The difference between the direct industrial and service corporate contribution to war fighting and peace-making in Afghanistan in the first decade of this century and operations in Iraq in 1991 could not be more stark and revelatory. Put simply, in little under 20 years industry has morphed from democracy's arsenal to its place as a critical component of the entire military instrument.[8]

Government and defence industrial interaction

The public and private companies that form the defence and security industrial base have been traditionally characterised by a specific taxonomy and set of labels. Certain companies are said to be 'prime' contractors if the specific business in question is the principal responsible delivery agent of a defence or security programme or project. That company, or indeed a completely separate one, could be labelled the 'original equipment manufacturer' (OEM) if it is the business which first designed and manufactured the equipment in question or maybe even simply purchased the licence from elsewhere to do so.[9]

Often supporting the 'prime' or 'OEM' is an extensive supply chain providing essential parts or services. The lead levels of these chains are often described as 'second tier' companies contributing towards the generation of defence capabilities. Bringing all of these constituent elements together is the role of a 'systems integrator' which may well be the prime contractor, the OEM (if different), or an advisory company specialising in programme or project management. For major items of equipment, there are normally many sub-layers of hundreds of suppliers, some of whom may not even be aware of the eventual destination of their products. There is also great variation among MoD suppliers as to the degree of their focus and dependence on the defence and wider security sector.

Of course, a globalised economy is marked by myriad actors and forces from the sole trader to multinational corporations. Stock exchanges are open to investors from around the world and a business may have owners in one country or many. Likewise, these companies can operate in many countries or have a business development pipeline to take goods and services to new international markets. Defence is no longer an exception to the economic dynamism associated with high modernity; most of the major UK defence and security firms employ large numbers of people beyond the shores of their 'home base' and provide goods and services to markets other than the national. Indeed, the UK government adopted a significant stance in the 2002 Defence Industrial Policy when it announced that any firm adding significant value in the UK would be treated as British. That meant that firms including Thales, Finmeccanica, Lockheed-Martin and General Dynamics could be defined as UK national entities, with this characterisation now being perceived as the norm.

Whilst defence and security businesses are subject to market forces and the economic cycle impacting upon other sectors, there is still a sense that the relationship between government and its national defence industry should be specialised and bespoke – to the extent that government could be said to, somehow, 'sponsor' the country's defence and security sector. As defence and national security present, in part, as highly technological phenomena, a government's role in the securing and prosecution of research, applied research and development of technologies applicable for military use seems significant, and is often too important to be left just to the dynamic of market forces.

Moreover, governments can place contracts with certain companies to ensure that an industrial capability is sustained in the mid- to long-term. Also, notions of industrial participation in the state and policies relating to 'offsets', taxation and broader societal investments made by industry may provide certain artefacts of government sponsorship. We could also point to modern concepts of partnering between government and businesses as a function of sponsorship whereby government shows a specific preference for a particular company (possibly post-competition), awarding it a long-term partnering contract for the provision of equipment or services, usually on an availability or output basis. Lastly, analysts often consider government support for exports as an overt example of government preference for, or sponsorship of, on-shore businesses in contrast to those registered in other countries.

Defence industries as economic imperative

It is helpful to consider the defence industrial output of the UK in the context of the wider economy. In terms of output as expressed by GDP, in 2010-2011 the largest sector was manufacturing at 17.5 per cent of the economy, with the wholesale and retail sector following at 10.5 per cent and financial services at 8.1 per cent. The defence industrial sector, by comparison, comprised just over one per cent of economic output.[10] Of MoD expenditure, in 2009, £13,387m was spent on the equipment and support programme (of which £6,669m was on capital infrastructure, £4,292m on equipment support and £2,426m on research and development).[11] This represented just over 40 per cent of the total defence budget, so we can say that approximately two per cent of GDP in the UK was consumed by defence activity with half of this used to purchase goods and services from commercial businesses.

These numbers provide some interesting signposts. Whilst the defence industrial base is self-evidently important to the UK economy, particularly in some regions and communities, on scale alone it is not as economically significant as the manufacturing, retailing or financial services sectors. Indeed, agriculture and extraction products and services represent three per cent of the economy and, as such, are three times the size of the defence industrial sector.

The private sector base on which a country depends for its defence capabilities may not be located entirely within its own territory, and clearly placing contracts overseas has important economic, foreign policy and defence implications. While the UK has stopped publishing data for identifiable defence imports, historically the UK has shipped-in about ten percent of its equipment needs.[12]

By way of an example, let us consider BAE Systems, the UK's largest defence company. Though, of course, seeing the company as simply a UK business is conceptually misplaced as it would be more accurate to describe it as a global defence and security corporation listed and headquartered in the UK. The company employs over 85,000 people worldwide and specialises in the research, development, design and manufacture of complex military and security equipment products, plus the preparation and support of the effective military deployment of equipment packages, typically involving the exploitation of complex technologies and electronic systems.

In terms of the UK, the operations of BAE Systems find employment for approximately 35,000 people, with almost half of these being professional engineers, either in practice or qualifying. Consequently, it is the UK's largest single private employer of engineers[13] which, in itself, hints at a substantial foundation of knowledge and intellectual capital residing in the UK under the banner of defence industries. Indeed, the UK part of the business generates revenues in the region of £9bn annually. An economic analysis[14] of the business highlighted that the company's direct value-added contribution to UK GDP was £3.3bn.[15] Moreover, productivity, as measured by value added per employee (or full time equivalent) was 85 per cent higher than the UK economic average.[16] The business, from its UK operations, generates net exports of £4.8bn and contributes £653m in direct taxation to the Exchequer. Interestingly, the research and development undertaken by this one business alone accounts for some £900m of new investment each year.

Furthermore, an estimated £4.1bn is spent on the procurement of equipment, components, materials and services from UK suppliers, and the company supports 125,000 jobs in the UK economy.[17] Extrapolating this analysis for the market as a whole, it can be deduced that more than 300,000 jobs in the United Kingdom service the defence and security market. This is significantly more than the total of all of the people serving in the armed forces.

National security skills and competencies within commerce and industry

Given that there are so many jobs within the UK dependent upon defence and security, it is helpful to consider the skills and competencies embedded within this workforce.

'Skills' can be defined as an individual's (or workforce's) expertise or practised ability derived from training and experience. 'Competencies', in contrast, are a shifting mix of qualifications, qualities, standards and assurances necessary to generate specific outputs or outcomes. A comprehensive skills and competencies economic profile is not maintained by the government, and trade associations related to defence keep only the broadest of subject-matter data. It may be necessary, therefore, to turn to a specific regional example to gain insight, but first some general thoughts.

Defence businesses, large and small, work right across the value chain from research, applied research and development activities through to repeat, unskilled or semi-skilled services such as grounds maintenance and catering within multi-activity support contracts. The range of skills and competencies utilised by the sector is truly staggering. Defence businesses provide both an occupational 'home' for engineers, scientists, designers, operational analysts, tradesmen and women, chefs, guards, hospitality professionals and maintenance staff, to list but some, and a portal for skilled and competent folk into the wider economy. Defence, therefore, should be conceptualised as a 'feeder' sector of skills and competencies into UK plc.

This is significant when it is recalled that the example of BAE Systems' contribution to the UK, discussed above, suggested that the company is the largest on-shore employer of engineering skills and competencies. This is just one defence business. The implication seems clear: defence companies are important repositories of national skills and employment opportunities. As well as being conceptually framed as part of the military instrument, these businesses seem integral to the UK's economic health, at least in the short to mid-term.

To expand upon this point, let us consider the role of the defence industrial hub at Barrow shipyard. Specialising in the design and manufacture of the UK's next generation of submarines, the site is the largest private employer in the whole of the Furness region, providing work for close to 5,000 full time (or equivalent) members of staff. The shipyard's supply chain embraces the whole of the UK with in excess of 1,200 suppliers commanding supply chain orders of close to £2bn. The site contributes £200m per annum to the regional economy in wages alone.

The skills profile of the site is modified annually by an intake of graduates and apprentices. More than 80 per cent of the latter are employed, trained and developed as skilled tradesmen and women working within the manufacturing cycle of the business. Most graduates, in comparison, are engineers and software specialists. They join a well-tuned graduate training scheme from which a quarter moves to non-defence sector businesses within five years. The rest seem to be retained within the defence and security market. In September 2010, over 150 graduates were employed along with close to 400 apprentices. This one site dominates its local economy but feeds into the larger national economy a high number of well-trained and developed professional staff on an ongoing basis. So Barrow generates key national security skills but also leverages broader competencies into the UK's macro-economy, and this is but one defence industrial site.

Conclusion

This short essay has made the conceptual case for the UK's defence and security businesses to be seen as both a component of the national military instrument and a key provider of skills and competencies to the economy. At a moment in history when multiple security hazards and risks are faced, including prolonged economic stagnation, developing suitable policies and approaches to sponsor and nurture this sector should be not simply a government priority but a principal obligation. As we approach the Strategic Defence and Security Review of 2015, it is hoped that this simple imperative will be realised.

The Evolution of Governance of National Security

Chris Donnelly

The governance of the UK has evolved over a long period and, as a result, is more complex and less obvious than that of many other democracies. Following the constitutional changes of the last Labour government, which have in the main been continued by the current Coalition, the past decade has seen a rapid evolution of this governance process which is still underway.

It was traditionally the case in the UK that the Cabinet played the primary role in deciding issues of national policy. Each new incoming government would re-establish, sometimes with changes, the Cabinet Committees which provide the day-to-day direction. Strong Cabinet government provided for a high degree of collaboration between ministers and departments (ministries) on all issues of national importance, informed by the Joint Assessment Staff and Joint Intelligence Committee within the Cabinet Office. Cabinet collective decision-making and responsibility encouraged ministers to be prepared to take risks as, except in the most extreme cases, responsibility for any failure would be shared with their colleagues, whereas success could actually bring advancement.

Under Prime Minister Tony Blair, the role of the Cabinet was reduced in favour of centralising power in the Prime Minister's office (a trend which continued under the Coalition government). This move away from Cabinet government towards a more presidential governmental style may have been politically expedient at the time, but it also had certain negative consequences. Firstly, deprived of the cover of collective Cabinet responsibility, ministers became increasingly unwilling to take any risk at all. Success could no longer lead to advancement, since Cabinet was effectively disempowered. Within their departments, civil servants likewise became more risk-averse. Innovation in policy-making ceased to be career-enhancing. Secondly, coherence and collaboration between government departments were lost. From this point on, cross-departmental working – as required by the 'comprehensive approach' – became ever more difficult. The loss of the Civil Service Staff College, latterly the National School of Government, removed the main tool for creating a language, culture and mechanism for inter-departmental dialogue and collaboration, and for sustaining research intra- and extramurally.

In an attempt to compensate for this loss of coherence, as well as to bring policy-making more under the direct control of the PM, policy was made primarily a Cabinet Office responsibility; departments were reduced to elaborating policy. To handle this, the size and power of the Cabinet Office were greatly increased. From being just a secretariat of the Cabinet with a staff of hundreds, the Cabinet Office became a large department in its own right, with over 3,000 staff.[1] In effect, it has become a Ministry of Ministries, with policy responsibilities and supervisory powers over other departments. It is today the greatest focus of power in the government after the PM. To exercise control in the new 'presidential' structure, the size of the PM's office also had to be increased from less than 200 staff to well over 1,000. The formal number of staff positions in both the PM's office and especially in the Cabinet Office understates their real size, as it does not include the agencies and subordinate offices set up to support the organisations. There has also been a dramatic growth in the number of lobbyists seeking influence over the Cabinet Office, and in the employment of selected advisors and consultants, rather than civil servants, to work in the Cabinet Office and its agencies. None of these people can be relied upon to 'speak truth unto power'.

At the same time, many of the practical executive functions of departments were hived off into agencies tasked with the delivery of policy (and often required to be financially viable). They merely had to deliver the contracted service, whether or not this proved possible or desirable. The large-scale removal of responsibility for both policy-making and policy delivery from the direct control of departments and ministers had certain inevitable consequences.

The first consequence was to detach policy-making from delivery – both previously done by one large, competent team within a department – making it very difficult to get timely feedback about the successes or failures of any policy as that policy came face-to-face with reality on implementation. As a result, it was now impossible to abort policies which proved unexpectedly bad, or to amend or fine-tune a policy to ensure that it could do what it had been intended to do. The essential 'bottom-up' input into policy was disabled. We began to see strings of successive policies, each hurriedly introduced in an attempt to correct the deficiencies of its predecessor. In an effort to correct this situation, the PM's office was given a *Delivery Unit* to enforce delivery of policies. Its effectiveness has remained, at best, dubious.

The second consequence was to weaken the technical, professional expertise of individual departments and remove the through-life career structure for civil servants within their departments. As a result, it not only reduced the attractiveness of the Civil Service as a profession but it began the steady decline of the technical competence of the Civil Service as a whole. It also resulted in a rapid erosion of the concept of 'integrity' in Crown Service, both civil and military, with the advent of private security services delivering what had hitherto been a Crown monopoly. An attitude that 'government could not trust Crown servants to innovate' and that 'bureaucracy was bad' came to prevail, when in fact this new approach simply fostered managerialism, reinforced by the new enthusiasm for performance management, about which more below.

The third consequence was to downgrade ministers from being 'improvers of the country through effective innovative policy' to becoming merely supervisors of contracts. The knock-on effect of this must ultimately impact upon the motivation of people to become MPs and members of the government.

The creation of the National Security Council (NSC) and the preparation of a National Security Strategy (NSS) reflected the need to compensate for the impact of these constitutional changes on departments concerned with national security. This happened at a time when the whole global security situation was in flux and national security was realised to be more than just the preserve of soldiers, diplomats, policemen and spies. Despite the then PM's insistence to the contrary, it was also becoming increasingly obvious that the UK's foreign policy was having a serious impact on the UK's domestic security. It was clearly no longer wise to deal with internal and external security issues as separate issues. The consequent need to improve the government's capacity to take a holistic view of national security and to implement a co-ordinated response provided a further strong impetus to create the NSS and NSC.

The Conservative Party's Green Paper on National Security[2] (published some six months before the last general election) had envisaged that the NSC, once established, would gradually develop into a body which could oversee and direct all aspects of national security, ensuring that coherent policy could be made in response to a holistic assessment (the NSS) and implemented by all relevant departments. The NSC would have bridged the gaps.

Had it developed in this way, the NSC would have become a very powerful institution. Logically, it would have developed its own secretariat – a 'headquarters' organisation to direct and co-ordinate the national effort – and a budget to facilitate the 'comprehensiveness' of multi-departmental working. However, this would have reduced the power of existing departments even further, challenging the new and growing predominance of the Cabinet Office and necessitating a fundamental reform of Whitehall. Consequently, the NSC has been diverted to evolve in a different direction. It has not grown; rather it has shrunk to the level and power of a Cabinet sub-committee. It functions today as a cross-departmental discussion forum, certainly useful, but without teeth of its own to do the job it was originally intended to do. As a result, in our national security, as within the rest of Whitehall, there is still no institution which can reverse the centrifugal trend diminishing the role of departments and pushing departments apart.

Another fundamental feature of governance in the UK since Victorian times has been the tradition of a strong, highly competent, non-political and uncorrupted body of Crown servants. Over the years, the institutions of the Crown had earned popular trust and were very effective. The interaction of the civil service with the national security agencies provided stability, freedom from political interference and a reputation for honesty and effectiveness on the part of all the agencies. There was strong positive identification between armed forces or police on the one hand, and the public on the other.

However, in the last decade the civil service, in particular, has changed fundamentally.[3] The impartiality, competence and altruism of the civil service have been reduced by a combination of political changes, shrinkage and inappropriate reforms. Most especially, the Blair reforms that changed the Crown servants in the civil and foreign services to *government* servants and the wholesale introduction of performance management have eroded the collective spirit which until then had inspired the civil service – the belief that civil servants were working for the Common Weal. Altruism has been replaced by a system which rewards individualistic ambition and stimulates competition between individuals, rather than building teams to compete with our enemies and competitors in pursuing the national interest.

Furthermore, the edict which made Crown servants into government servants means that parliament cannot now be advised independently by the civil service, the foreign service or the disciplined services. Government servants are only allowed to put forward the government's line, and must implement government policies obediently, even if they disagree with them. Where now is the concept of 'speaking truth unto power?' The opposition is no longer informed adequately to propose constructive alternatives to government proposals. It can do no more than indulge in poorly-informed, negative attacks that do nothing to inspire the confidence of the electorate in the competence of their representatives.

These factors have contributed to a loss of public confidence in government generally. The reduction in power of the civil service, and the reduction in size and technical competence of many departments (especially defence), gave rise in turn to the creation of the senior civil service (SCS). This compounded the problems because it was established as an elite of individuals 'with management expertise' – managerialists rather than people expert and experienced in the specifics of their departments. This, coupled with the closed nature of the SCS (accessible only through a fast-stream process of accelerated promotion through management posts), has created a two-tier civil service with a separate SCS primarily loyal to itself and to its own institutional interests, directly serving the interests of their ministers rather than the national interest, as was the case in the past.

The problem with any such closed elite is that its main motivation will always be to maintain its own power and position. Promotion within this closed elite is horizontal, i.e. between departments. To justify its monopolising of all the top posts, the SCS has had to establish that special domain competence is not necessary to run a department and, consequently, technically competent people can be demoted. The evolution of the leadership of the MoD over the past two years provides an excellent, if unedifying, example of this process at work. The transformation of the scientific advisors from independent competent advisors to ministers to politically appointed senior civil servants with, in the case of MoD, budgets to ensure they lack any credible independence, is merely an example of the irrelevance of departments.

As the civil service has been reduced in size and technical, professional competence, it has been less and less able to undertake technical tasks from within its own resources. To compensate, it has relied more and more on calling in consultants. This trend is reinforced by the (unsubstantiated) belief – in some quarters almost an ideology – that introducing commercial business practices is the answer to 'administrative inefficiency'. This belief is held in ignorance of the root causes of the current problem. It also conveniently ignores the fundamental differences between business and government, especially in the security sector. It makes a god of *efficiency*, forgetting the fundamental importance for government of *effectiveness*, especially as far as national security issues are concerned. In the complex world of security, it is fitness-for-purpose within the current security environment that must be judged, not an irrelevant set of 'business metrics' based on past requirements. A strong, competent and confident Crown service can make good use of consultants if it controls them well. But a managerialist bureaucracy which is no longer technically literate, which goes to consultants not just for answers but for help in posing the questions, is no longer fit-for-purpose.

The UK's long tradition of a strong, competent, honest administration has left many people with a confidence in today's civil service that is no longer wholly justified. This is not to say that there are no good civil servants. There are a great many. Indeed sincere, competent dedicated individuals are probably in the majority at every level. But the *system* no longer functions as it should and is in need of drastic reform.

However, because of the strong legacy of our civil service, the role of parliament as the third element of the system of governance in the UK has been relatively poorly developed in past years. To date, the parliamentary select committees have had little power – nothing to compare with the power of a US Congressional committee. Nor do they have the structured oversight responsibilities enjoyed by their counterparts in, say, Canada or Germany. Lacking real power, parliamentary committees have been left only with the ability to 'name and shame' as a tool of democratic oversight. But in today's networked world, it is surely better to forestall a disaster rather than point the finger of blame after it has happened. The time would seem to be ripe to review and perhaps to enhance the power and responsibility of parliament, making security a parliamentary responsibility as 'representative owner' to compensate for the deficiencies developing elsewhere in our system of governance. Issues concerning national security should not be merely party political matters, for the timescales they cover span many election cycles.

A further element in the UK's system of governance has been the role played by the academic and journalistic world. Again, this was never as strong or as influential as in the USA and it has grown weaker in the past decade. But it is still extremely important, not least as a means by which the public is kept informed about national security issues and about the agencies responsible for its preservation. But here too, the past 15 years have seen significant changes. The Research Assessment Exercise, introduced to measure and evaluate research excellence in universities, has had the perverse effect of discouraging imaginative forward thinking in defence and national security issues at precisely the time when such thinking is desperately needed because it is no longer being produced in government and military circles. The uncontrollable growth of the internet, the proliferation of social networking, the fall in the quality of classic journalism and the loss of technically competent journalists has created a public information environment which is now very difficult for government and parliament to cope with. The very frequency of leaks and exposures acts against transparency in government and generates an unhealthy secrecy.

Government bodies – and parliament in particular – therefore, have a responsibility to provide leadership and guidance to academia, think tanks and the media as to the issues they should be researching. It takes courage for political leaders and civil servants to invite alternative views or models of the future and to encourage in-depth research which may contradict current policies. But an effective 'challenge process' is a pre-requisite for successful governing. There is far too little of such *loyal challenge* in Whitehall today, despite the lip-service often paid to it.

'Risk' and governance in the UK today

Risk management has been a very harmful obsession for the past two decades. This attitude to risk has become a pernicious ideology which has now so thoroughly permeated our thinking and shaped our attitudes and practices that it is accepted as normal. Risk management has become a huge, profitable industry with practitioners, clients, qualifications and courses – all the trappings of permanence and respectability.

This approach to risk emerged from a variety of sources from the late 1980s onwards. It owes a great deal to EU employment legislation, health and safety legislation, 'precautionary principles' and performance management concepts. It was reinforced by litigation practices introduced from the USA. An assessment of its impact on our ability to advance UK interests indicates that it has significantly reduced UK competitiveness in the global hypercompetition.

The drastic changes following the end of the Cold War, the downsizing of the armed forces, the collapse of industry, including the defence industry, in the UK and the introduction of the practice of rewarding civil servants for 'shedding risk' (e.g. transferring the risks of new weapons development from the state to the manufacturer), all brought the issue firmly into Whitehall. By the early 1990s, 'risk' had in effect been defined in the civil service as something totally bad rather than something which presents both a threat and an opportunity.

In fact, risk is a natural, indeed an essential, element of evolution and adaptation. Everyone who undertakes research accepts the risk of failure as necessary to create something new, whether knowledge or artefact; everyone who attempts a work of art accepts risk as a stimulus to creativity. By definition, any *decision* involves some level of risk. Only those who manage but have no association with the outcome fear risk, as it exposes their incompetence. We should also pose the philosophical question: 'Can risk itself actually be managed?' Risk can and should be assessed. The *consequences* of risk can be managed, certainly – but risk itself?

As the 1990's progressed, the idea of risk being all bad grew in both the civilian and military bureaucracies in MoD.[4] The 'peacetime' mindset of the public and the steady loss of technical expertise in national security issues in public bodies, parliament and the media added to the 'risk-averse' culture that was growing in the UK. This culture has been reinforced in the past decade by the move away from Cabinet government with its collective responsibility, as well as by other government policies, and by the emergence of a new media environment. This environment has made government control of information impossible. Official, verified information today can never hope to compete with the speed of personal witness from the 'citizen journalist' or the Al Qaida ideologue. 'Trial and error' began to be replaced by 'error and trial-by-media'.

For national security this last issue is a particularly unfortunate trend. The effect has been to make people negative and defensive, to encourage them to avoid anything which might conceivably have a harmful effect. Our institutions are no longer trying to do anything, they are just trying to stop things happening and to be as comfortable as possible. They create the illusion that this is 'security'. It is not. It is stagnation, which is the biggest risk of all – 'playing safe' is today just too risky.

The big challenge now for the UK's broader security establishment, and in particular for its acquisition process, is how to redefine 'risk' and take 'risk management' off the agenda. It is damaging to the competitive stance which the UK needs. How do we replace this disastrous negative mindset with one which encourages people to be positive and proactive, to seize an opportunity, to be driven by an ethos of 'advancing the UK's interests' so that our country can find its place in a rapidly changing world? How to reintroduce the competitive stance?

We can start by questioning the basic assumptions and re-defining the word 'risk' as something potentially good. Not that we wish to encourage foolhardiness, but rather on the basis that the famous regimental motto 'Who dares wins' is historically proven to be accurate. We can reward people who take risks instead of penalising them, on the basis that we will generally get the behaviour we reward. We can do away with a lot of inappropriately applied and restrictive health and safety legislation. We can amend our training and education programmes.

Eliminating risk management may not be so forbidding a task as many might think. The practice has been questioned for some years in the commercial world, where there is a growing recognition that it has been grossly overdone and that the tools of the trade (such as 'balanced score cards') have been misused and abused, applied to circumstances for which they were never intended.

A dispassionate analyst of the current National Security Strategy process might conclude that risk-management is today nothing more than a defensive mechanism used by those in power to share, and thereby avoid, blame. Blame is shuffled off to risk managers or 'senior responsible owners'. When MoD civil servants 'shed risk', for example in the acquisition process, the risk they are shedding is *political* risk. The risk that is inserted into equipment programmes, e.g. by their inadequate investment in R&D, may no longer fall on their heads. But it will ultimately be borne by the user of that equipment – the soldier, who my pay for it with his life.

Whitehall's Strategic Deficit

Jonathan Shaw

Whitehall doesn't do strategy. Not only does Whitehall not do strategy, Whitehall can't even agree what strategy is. Just after the last election, the Parliamentary Public Administration Select Committee did an investigation into Whitehall's grand strategy. Bernard Jenkin, the Chairman, asked every attendee for their definition of strategy and got almost as many different answers as he had interviewees. The lack of agreement on terminology undermined the subsequent interviews.

As George Orwell wrote in *Politics and the English Language*: 'If thought corrupts language, language can also corrupt thought.'[1] Without clarity about language, clarity of thought is impossible and misunderstandings encouraged.

I still think that our public services attract a disproportionate amount of talent to their ranks; we are lucky in the UK with our political class. The problem is that they are ill-equipped by experience or training for the executive role demanded of them, so there is a skills gap.

And then there is the structural problem: Whitehall is set up for departmental delivery of departmental responses. It has to bend itself out of shape to do cross-Whitehall governmental responses, precisely the responses that the original NSS in 2008 said would be the norm if UK was to meet future security challenges. In the absence of any cross-Whitehall doctrine or executive methodology, Whitehall pretty much makes it up as it goes along. It is this absence of sound methodology and precise language that makes fools of us all.

But, you will protest, Whitehall has the reputation of being one of the most joined-up civil services in the western world. The frightening thing is that I would agree with that. Whitehall achieves what it does due to the quality of the people, their innate pragmatism and service culture, and the physical construction of Whitehall, described by a previous Chief of Defence Staff, General Walker, as 'a street designed to run an Empire'.

Indeed the executive picture of Whitehall has some very bright spots, such as its ability to handle counter-terrorism (CT) incidents. Whitehall handles CT incidents better than any other capital I have seen, Washington and Paris in particular. The handling of the 7/7 crisis was as good as you will get for an incident such as that, drawing on a long tradition of excellence in this area. But the Whitehall domestic security world works so well for a number of reasons largely peculiar to itself:

- its personnel are practitioners as well as policy experts, and they bring their executive training with them

- the Command and control is well established and exercised

- those involved are used to working together and have compatible and well understood cultures and methodologies

- those involved have an executive attitude to risk, used to taking decisions in conditions of uncertainty to get ahead of events.

These qualities are more or less lacking across the rest of Whitehall.

Jack Straw, as Home Secretary, was so impressed by what he saw of this CT system in Cabinet Office briefing room (COBR) during the Spring 2000 Afghan hostage crisis that when, in September 2000, the fuel protest required his handling, he re-convened COBR – and was dismayed when it didn't work. This was because policy experts from across Whitehall were thrust into an executive environment for which they had no training or experience. Furthermore, the pace of the three-day crisis outstripped the ability of Whitehall to create coordination or to react to events, let alone get ahead of them. In the end, the fuel protest was not won by Whitehall, it was lost by the protesters who unwittingly had chosen the 'nuclear option', i.e. they had no intermediary negotiating postures and, faced with imminent national breakdown (including deaths in hospitals for which they would be held responsible), they took their finger off the button.

Worse was to follow in the foot and mouth disease crisis of 2001, which overwhelmed the ability of Whitehall to coordinate the national response. Whitehall recognised its executive failing and called in the army's 101 Logistic Brigade Headquarters to coordinate the government's efforts from the Ministry of Agriculture. This the army did, filling the executive deficit of Whitehall by applying a language, methodology and discipline across departmental activity. So alien was this approach to some that, according to one civilian participant I spoke to, the key to successful execution appeared to be to make sure everyone turned up five minutes early for a brief, make a map bird-table around which everyone gathered and make everyone stand up during briefs. If only life were that simple!

Meanwhile, inside COBR, at the start of one morning of particular crisis, a certain minister looked plaintively at the assembled officials and declared, with commendable honesty: 'I'm sorry, you are looking to me for leadership, but I am completely untrained for this role.' The minister concerned could well have been speaking for increasing numbers of politicians whose experience is increasingly political and hence decreasingly executive. Senior civil servants today share the same problem. Yet power and leadership are notoriously complex to master; they require training and experience. All of this suggests structural, methodological and training shortfalls in the Whitehall system.

'But,' I hear you cry, 'surely we have come a long way in the last ten years, with the creation of the much vaunted *comprehensive approach*.' Much has been achieved under this banner, particularly latterly on the ground in Afghanistan. But we would have been much better served if we had had a comprehensive plan. For it was the absence of a national plan that led to what I saw as so much incoherence in both Afghanistan on the counter narcotics ticket and in Iraq when I commanded in Basra in 2007. At its best, the comprehensive approach has allowed departmental action to be coordinated on the ground to good national effect. At its worst, it has provided a political smokescreen, an illusion of coherence, whilst allowing departmental independence to dominate over government intent. The sum of government action needs to be more than the sum of its individual parts. At present, there is no mechanism to cohere these individual parts and to add the value you get from conjoined action.

Let me give a grossly simplified illustration of the creation of cross-government activity as I have witnessed it.

- a problem is identified

- departments offer activity in pursuit of addressing this problem

- the government's PR people then announce that the government has identified a problem it will address by the following departmental activity

- No 10 is happy, the departments are happy, the PR and media message people are happy – until it is found that this voluntary and un-cohered activity does not actually amount to a plan

There are gaps between departmental activities; some work together, some are disconnected, others contradict each other. Few endure to achieve the unified desired effect over time on the problem.

Time now to put my money where my mouth is and define my terms when I talk of strategy.

Let's start on familiar ground, with Clausewitz, who famously defined strategy in terms of 'ends, ways and means'. My observation is that this can all too often be interpreted from our perspective only; to wit:

- these are the ends which we are pursuing

- these are our means which we are going to deploy

- these are the ways in which we are going to deploy them

The vital player missing from this UK government-centric misinterpretation of 'ends, ways and means' is the *enemy*; and the enemy has a vote, as we have been reminded in Iraq and Afghanistan, and will be reminded again in Africa and the Middle East. Consequently, we need to adapt Clausewitz in seeing strategy as the constant process of cohering policy (the objectives) with reality (the object of one's policy) and resource (the assets, most importantly including time, required to close the gap).

Policy is decided upon at the strategic level, reality is grappled with at the tactical level.

Critically and least understood, resource is allocated at an intermediate level known in the military as the 'operational' level. This is a level of command, not just a coordinating function. It is this level of command that no longer exists in Whitehall.

I am told this role used to be filled by what is still officially called the Central Department, but is now more commonly known as the Treasury. I understand it had authority not just over finance but also over the coherence of departmental actions. However, the Treasury's cohering authority fell victim to the Blair/Brown conflict, and the Cabinet Office has never been authorised to fill this command role. It still only has coordinating, not directing, authority. This has removed a vital level of command without which Whitehall will struggle to create, and can never hope to execute, strategy.

Let me emphasise the constant process required to execute strategy over time. It is a constant process of cohering, as there are changes in reality, as resources change or face competing priorities, and as the original policy goals come under challenge. The political damage of altering policy goals during a campaign makes it all the more important to choose achievable policy goals at the outset. As our political class gets less experienced in what is and is not achievable in the real world, so policy objectives are more likely to tend to the politically desirable than to the actually achievable. Perhaps we should pay more heed to the advice of Douglas Hurd, writing in 1997 on his lessons from the Balkans: 'Do not proclaim in public what you hope to accomplish until you are confident that you can carry it through. Be prepared to say no, to stay out unless and until you have that confidence and share it with the main actors.'[2]

Having set realistic goals, a feedback loop between the policy, reality and resources needs to be established to keep these three in balance over time.

Cabinet government might once have been capable of executing strategy as described. But in recent years it has struggled to cope with the increasing responsibility of government, the increasing cross-departmental working required to discharge this responsibility, and the 24/7 media demand and speed of modern communications. The resulting trend towards the centralising of policy making on No10 has combined with the demise of the Central Department's cohering role. The demise of Cabinet has reduced departmental ministers to executors of others' policy, and the feedback loop that is so essential to strategy execution has been lost. Policy is now disconnected from execution and there is no operational level command to address the resource issues.

As No 10's dominance has grown, the disincentives to speak truth to power in Whitehall have also grown. I recall a bizarre moment in the foot and mouth crisis, where it became clear that the cost of saving an industry worth millions was going to run into the billions. No minister could be found to tell the PM this, and so no challenge was made to the policy pledge to support the farmers, no matter what.

Such disincentives to honesty invite perverted behaviours by Departments, and it could perhaps be understood if they sought advantage within a flawed policy rather than to challenge it; Whitehall is, after all, a battleground for resources.

To conclude, there is a consensus that Whitehall could do better. The challenge is how to get Whitehall to improve its cross-departmental capability to conceive and execute strategy. I believe it should be possible to create a cross-Whitehall doctrine and executive methodology and to train all in the Whitehall village in its execution, without bringing Whitehall to its knees.

More ambitiously, the central department should be re-empowered to direct finance and cohere activity to provide that missing operational level of command between policy and execution. A rationalisation of departments on leaner functional lines would lead to better integrated government action and a reduced bill in line with current austerity measures. For all this to happen, it will take a concerted effort by us all to light that bonfire that so many observers of Whitehall have built under current structures and practices.

A New Acquisition Process to Acquire What We Need From What We Have Got Available

Alan Macklin

Introduction

If we were to agree that the current acquisition system is broken, what would 'good' look like? It would be very tempting to start with a clean piece of paper but, in seeking to offer an approach that has practical application, we must anchor ourselves in reality – whilst not being averse to constructive challenge – and avoid the temptation to throw the baby out with the bathwater. The key components of the title are assessed to be 'from what we have got available' and 'what we need'. The former plays to the realm of portfolio management and the latter to the realm of programme management which would then set the scene for individual project acquisition decisions.

What we have available: portfolio perspective

Portfolio management is a well-established activity in government departments and is a 'science' of which the characteristics and skill-sets necessary to deliver 'good' are relatively new. The Office of Government Commerce (OGC) launch of Portfolio, Programme and Project Management (P3M), with the seven perspectives of its maturity model, represented 'new' thinking in 2008: the Good Practice Guide to portfolio management,[1] launched in 2011, was then an evolution of this work. This evolution brings with it the imperative to think more deeply about portfolio management as a disciplined science with tools, techniques and evaluation criteria. The very welcome introduction of an explicit provision for risk and contingency into the MoD's equipment plan is a significant step on the route to a new model. Having set out the portfolio stall, the next step is to ensure that decision-making, supported by appropriate data, demonstrably supports the objectives of this portfolio. The best portfolios are managed as a set of sub-portfolios and programmes with discrete objectives, leaving individual projects embedded at subordinate levels.

One of the key disciplines of good portfolio management is the clarity of boundaries and the delegation of authority and responsibility to the appropriate level. There is a real dilemma here, with portfolio management all too often in the hands of boards who operate on lifecycles (frequently annual or electoral cycles) that are much shorter than the lifecycles of their component programmes and projects. The secret is to set processes in place to prevent portfolio management disrupting programme and project plans. A good example of how this might be achieved was demonstrated by the removal of the Bank of England from day to day political control. This provides the precedent for giving freedom of action to a body that needs to take long term decisions at programme level by insulating it from shorter-term political imperatives. Such an approach should be adopted in the new model for acquisition.

Portfolio management also operates at the level above defence: government management of its overall portfolio and the distribution of resources between departments. At a time of fiscal crisis and no perceived existential threat, resources allocated to defence can be considered 'discretionary' in the same manner as the allocation of resources to law and order, education, health or welfare. The secret of good portfolio management is to ensure that the expectations raised and capabilities required are aligned with the resources allocated. This is a higher level aspect of the factors involved in a new model for acquisition but, given the lead times for the most complex defence projects, portfolio management decisions at government level need to be informed by the potentially significant impact on strategic projects.

What we need: programme perspective

'What we need?' is a question that must be addressed in a holistic manner. Drawing on the OGC's P3M model, the first step is to identify the key stakeholders at each level of disaggregation, starting from the top, in order to gain agreement on the desired outcomes to be achieved: and at a time of discretionary defence capability, this stakeholder group goes much wider than the military. The example of the London 2012 Olympic Park carries lessons for defence in terms of identifying programme outcomes that are pre-requisites for project delivery success. In the Olympic Park case, the key stakeholders signed up to a set of programme goals that addressed their needs and that had no direct relationship to the delivery of a major sporting event in summer 2012. Those programme goals shaped the design and delivery of the individual projects without fundamentally undermining the tactical 'capabilities' delivered at project level. Different nations have different ways of achieving this stakeholder support: in the USA, the F35 Joint Strike Fighter is known as the 'un-cancellable project' because stakeholder analysis led Lockheed Martin to develop design and construction plans that commit to work-share in 48 states of the Union – effectively guaranteeing support across Congress.

There are many who will decry an approach that appears to subordinate the needs of the warfighter to wider stakeholder interests. But this is to misunderstand the difference between programme goals and project deliverables. The delivery of the Olympic Park venues to performance, time and cost was achieved *because* those wider programme goals were satisfied in delivering the project outputs. A project-by-project approach to each venue in isolation would have led to squabbles and challenges by groups with vested interests and delay would have been imposed by those who wanted to be confident about the 'bigger picture' but could not obtain that confidence in the early submissions. The question 'what do we need?' should not be targeted, in the first place, simply at the armed forces.

If we need to consider a 'higher level' than military need, where should we look? The first places are government strategy and then, in light of that strategy, at the defence enterprise rather than the military alone. In the same way that 'capability management' recognised the need to look through the five lenses of: military capability, finance, commercial, research & technology and industry when considering how to deliver a project, so must 'what we need' be looked at through the five 'grand strategic' lenses of UK capability: defence, economic (and fiscal), technology, industrial (both sovereign and competitive) and diplomacy/influence – with timescales measured in decades rather than years. This perspective brings us back to the disconnection between the timescale for acquisition strategic planning and that for the electoral cycle. This is not new and means to tackle the challenge are evidenced in the model for the Bank of England and the intent behind the National Infrastructure Plan.[2]

In the 1999 Smart Acquisition initiative, McKinsey's work with the 'Equipment Capability Customer', attempted to embrace the programme level perspective of UK defence capability and, under different circumstances, could have led to programme level planning across many of the grand strategic lenses. Unfortunately this was incompatible with stated industrial policy, the construct of the procurement organisation and MoD financial structures at that time. The current Defence Reform Programme, with the transfer of financial delegations to the front line commands, and conversion of Defence Equipment and Support (DE&S) to a bespoke trading entity, provides an alignment of transformational initiatives that offers tantalising prospects of a new model for acquisition at the programme level that builds on many of features that were stillborn in Smart Acquisition.

Building on the principles outlined above, a new model would entail a clear delineation of the portfolio boundaries with appropriate principles & strategies articulated (not necessarily in the public domain) for each of the grand strategic lenses. Within this construct would run the programmes whose goals (not project solutions) would be signed up to by the appropriate key stakeholders. This is no easy matter as defence acquisition is highly complex and there are multiple programme dimensions whose integration and trade-offs will require programme management skills of the very highest order. It is only within this established structure that project detail should be considered. It is fully recognised that political and media headlines are made of sound-bites at a level of detail out of proportion to the bigger picture: and this is precisely why the new model requires project detail to be insulated, as far as possible, from short term headlining and day-to-day political influence. In the new model, projects would be assessed against their compliance with and contribution to the relevant programme goals, in a manner akin to the 'arm's length' approach taken to the Bank of England's day-to-day decision making. Such a model requires the acceptance of some fundamentally new behaviours and approaches to project delivery but this is not a leap into the unknown as the Olympic Park and Bank of England provide many good precedents.

International alternatives

In considering a new model, it is insightful to reflect on other approaches adopted around the world and to reflect on the circumstances that led to their decisions. In the USA, when Special Operations Command (SOCOM) was formed in 1987, the Department of Defense placed all special operation forces (army, navy, air force) under one four-star command. Unlike the other unified commands (e.g. EUCOM, PACOM, CENTCOM) and functional commands (e.g. TRANSCOM), the SOCOM commander was given independent budget and acquisition authority: he had authority to buy anything he desired off the shelf or through the regular acquisition process. SOCOM established a single-source acquisition programme manager, answerable to the four-star commander, with authority to provide the weapons and service support across the service lines of authority (Seals, Rangers, Green Beret, AF Special Tactics) required by the SOCOM commander's strategic guidance. This included authority to buy equipment off the shelf and authorise weapons development. This offers an example of exclusive focus on the military capability strategic lens and, it can be argued, is only sustainable because the other lenses can be addressed in the wider Department of Defence acquisition programmes.

In France, whose military culture is probably closest to the UK's in Europe, the acquisition model reflects the same grand strategic lenses. However the French approach places a greater primacy on French industrial capability – and through that to its economic capability – with the detailed military requirement having a less prominent role.

The European Union Organisation for Joint Armament Cooperation (OCCAR) model is another very different approach that seeks to drive benefit from commonality and reduce the overheads of running individual national procurement authorities. Experience suggests that this model has its benefits (and many dis-benefits) as a procurement model but suffers many of the shortcomings of the eurozone in terms of lack of alignment of programme outcomes and shortfalls in the ability to achieve timely executive decision-making.

These alternative models are perfectly viable and reflect a different balance between the five grand strategic lenses from that currently adopted in UK. The UK has clear and distinctive imperatives as a nation:

- whose armed forces are intended for use in pursuit of national interests around the globe

- for which defence exports are a material component of the national economy

- whose strategic & trade links make diplomacy/ influence a significant part of the national agenda

These all mean that the international alternatives appear to fail to satisfy our needs. We need to develop a model that allows our particular balance between the five lenses to be addressed. This requires the balance to be articulated, at least inside government, and the desired outcomes to be articulated at the very highest level in order to optimise the model to support those outcomes.

Reflection

Recent UK experiences outside the defence domain offer us insights into what a new model for defence acquisition might look like, building on proven ideas and techniques and clearly articulated desired outcomes at the highest level. The bigger scale of change lies in our preparedness to embrace these ideas. The Defence Reform Programme offers a unique opportunity for transformation – in head office, in the front line commands and in DE&S – to realise the benefits that can only be achieved if this scale of change is embraced across the defence portfolio. As we have seen over the years, in an environment where only one variable seeks to move within a grid where all other points are heavily constrained, progress can only ever be incremental. Are we brave enough, within and well beyond the MoD, to seize this unique opportunity?

Based on their data, the Standish researchers propose that pursuing an iterative series of smaller, evolutionary projects is a more effective way to develop and deliver critical capabilities than establishing large, slow, expensive programmes designed to provide a single-step-to-capability. My book provides further examples of FIRE in action, then identifies the principles and practices involved. The objective is to help equip decision-makers with tools that help move projects in the direction of speed, thrift, simplicity and restraint.

Critically, the FIRE approach can be implemented without radically redesigning the acquisition process, publishing mountains of new policy or instituting any new laws. Because it focuses on the day-to-day decisions made by practitioners, decision-makers can apply it within virtually any regulatory environment and any organisation, simply by pursuing opportunities to restrain cost, schedule and complexity. FIRE can also be applied to the policy, and should be, but that need not be the starting point. As a general rule, good policy tends to lag good practice, which means a lack of policy is not an insurmountable barrier to implementation.

A brief example may help show how FIRE works. Let's consider two fighter jets which the US Air Force successfully developed in the early 1970's: the F-15 Eagle and the F-16 Fighting Falcon.

Both jets were developed under the same policy environment and were subjected to the same laws. In compliance with the established process, both programs published a Statement of Work (SOW), describing to industry the required attributes of the aircraft to be built. This is where their approaches diverged. The F-15's SOW was 250 pages long, while the F-16's was only 25 pages – an order of magnitude smaller.

Contractor proposals for the Eagle weighed in at nearly 2,000 pages, and awarding the contract took the better part of a year. That sounds remarkably fast by today's standards, but not when compared with its contemporary, the F-16. Proposals to build the Fighting Falcon were limited to 60 pages and the contract was awarded in less than three months. According to Col James Burton's calculations in his book *The Pentagon Wars*, the F-16 was delivered in half the time, for half the cost of the F-15.

The point of that story is simply that military acquisition programmes do not have to cost so much, take so long and be so complicated. As the F-16 shows, programme managers generally have the option to constrain the cost, complexity and schedule associated with awarding a contract. Bear in mind, the request for proposal (RFP) is only one minor aspect of the larger acquisition effort. That is, the F-16's short RFP is merely a sign of a wider, deeper preference for focused restraint, while the F-15's longer documents are symptomatic of the programme's overall ethos which placed an unnecessary premium on complexity, both in terms of the technology and the paperwork.

The F-15 team could arguably have opted for a shorter, more focused set of documentation, which would have reduced the cost and time associated with that effort, had the leaders chosen to pursue speed, thrift, simplicity and restraint. The fact that they did not do so has everything to do with culture and nothing at all to do with policy or procedure. While the Eagle is a fine aircraft with a long and proud heritage, it is not clear the F-15 delivered twice as much value as the equally proud F-16, despite expending twice as much time and money.

Just as spending a lot of time and money on the Eagle did not cause a commensurate increase in its value, the tight constraints on time, money and complexity did not reduce the F-16's suitability and effectiveness. In fact, the USAF Fact Sheet says the Fighting Falcon's 'manoeuvrability and combat radius... exceed that of all potential threat fighter aircraft'. The US Air Force expects to get upwards of 50 years of service from that particular jet, proving that speed and thrift are not incompatible with a long service life.

It bears repeating that nothing in federal law or acquisition policy required the Falcon team to write such a short RFP, nor was the Eagle team forced to write such a long one. It was simply a matter of one group placing a premium on speed and simplicity, demonstrating strong technical leadership to focus the effort on the most important functions, while the other had no such focus. The lesson is that this approach is immediately available to any leader who chooses to apply it. If leaders at the national level decide to encourage and reward FIRE-style approaches, the resulting combination of cost savings and improved operational effectiveness is potentially tremendous.

To paraphrase Nassim Taleb from his book *Antifragile*,[4] the status quo appears inevitable when viable alternatives are not readily visible. Accordingly, a FIRE initiative aims to enhance the visibility of high-speed, low-cost alternatives by telling stories like the F-16, expanding awareness of what is possible and equipping practitioners and leaders at all levels of responsibility with the tools necessary to pursue these alternatives.

In fact, many of the most impactful tools are already in our toolbox. Just as every programme manager can write a 21-page RFP if they chose to do so, every government contract establishes a variety of incentives to reward various outcomes. Clearly, the concept of a contractual incentive requires no great mental leap. What FIRE proposes is to establish contractual incentives that reward speed, thrift, simplicity and restraint instead of the current incentives which tend to perversely reward cost growth and schedule delays, despite all protests to the contrary.

Consider the following: in 1998, NASA cancelled the Clark satellite programme because its projected cost growth exceeded the 15 per cent threshold established in its contract. Nothing in the law or policy required NASA to establish the threshold, nor is there any formal barrier to prevent today's military acquisition leaders from following their example. The reason Clark's termination clause was established – and executed – had nothing to do with policy and everything to do with the culture of 'Faster, Better, Cheaper' (FBC) that NASA's leaders fostered during the 1990's. In that culture, cancellation was preferable to cost growth. This shaped the way people led programmes, wrote contracts, executed procedures and implemented policies. Incidentally, some of NASA's proudest moments occurred during the FBC era, including the Pathfinder mission to Mars which was developed in half the time and one fifteenth the budget of the 1970s Viking Mars mission.

This transformation to a FBC culture did not happen overnight, nor was it easy. Administrator Dan Goldin introduced FBC to NASA in 1992 and 'experienced significant difficulties' along the way, according to Professor Howard McCurdy's book on the topic.[5] The Standish Group researchers echo that observation, writing 'It is very clear that reducing scope and breaking up large projects [into small projects] are difficult tasks.'

Despite the difficulty, the Standish report offers the encouraging observation that 'the rewards and benefits are quickly evident when the organisation starts to receive value early in the project cycle'. Their conclusion, which I emphatically agree with, is simply that 'there is no need for large projects'. Reducing project size may not be easy, but it is certainly possible. This means the big, expensive, slow alternative is both undesirable and unnecessary.

The important question is how to create a similar culture within government organisations today. The short answer is that this culture cannot be created, at least not by fiat. The good news is that it does not have to be created because it already exists.

The innovative FIRE culture is obviously not ubiquitous throughout the government, but within any formal organisation of significant size we can easily find small teams of innovators hard at work developing affordable systems that are available when needed and effective when used. These small teams often operate below the radar, largely unrecognised and unrewarded, but they exist and are doing fantastic work. This is where a visionary leader can make a tremendous difference. As with the existing tools which need only be picked up and used, leaders can start by encouraging the preferred culture and fostering its expansion from where it already resides into areas where it is not yet established.

These small groups become cultural ambassadors, the archetypes of cool and the model for other teams to emulate. As leaders use FIRE to cast a vision of rapid, thrifty innovation, these small groups also serve as evidence that such performance is not merely possible in a theoretical sense but is indeed happening as we speak. Newcomers to the approach are presented with the option of joining in or being left behind. This is how culture spreads and how change happens.

To further encourage widespread adoption, it is helpful to incorporate FIRE principles and tools into the training curriculum, encouraging the workforce to develop and hone their ability to use methods like TRIZ, Lean, Agile and the Simplicity Cycle. This is a key aspect of increasing people's awareness of the FIRE alternative. Fortunately, a significant amount of training material, including academic research papers and classroom lectures, is already available

Of course, measuring performance is critical to any improvement effort, so it is helpful to establish a set of FIRE-oriented metrics. These measurements should assess whether speed, thrift, simplicity and restraint are being pursued in our programmes, then provide rewards accordingly. This is easily done once FIRE is accepted as a foundation, and in fact several FIRE-friendly metric sets are already developed and available for use.

Incorporating and adopting the principles, tools, training and metrics of the FIRE approach will help ensure our ability to provide agile, efficient responses to the unpredictable challenges ahead. They are well documented, field-tested and already implemented in some places. A willing leader who wants to implement FIRE will find an enthusiastic cohort ready to help bring the concept to bear on a large scale.

Achieving Successful Transformation of MoD: The Principles and Practice of Reforming National Defence and Security Organisations

Henry Strickland

Introduction

As defence cost inflation and shrinking budgets bite harder, the UK, like many NATO member and partner nations, is facing not just a downsizing of its national defence system but a fundamental restructuring. Models of military and defence organisation which worked well at a given scale will not function at much smaller scales. New models need to be devised and introduced. This is always difficult and, if it is not tackled properly, the process can be disastrous for the armed forces and for the nation.

Changing an organisation is difficult, because people dislike change. It forces them out of their comfort zone and requires them to think for themselves, rather than mindlessly following routine. Serious change can take a long time to work through an organisation (anything up to five years). It will be a messy and disruptive process. It can cost at least five times the original budget. If the change is tackled as a one-off, top-down imposition, then, even if it succeeds, it will have to be repeated in five years' time because the world will have moved on, and the result is likely to be perpetually chasing after a chimera. Consequently, if serious change needs to be undertaken by MoD then it is well worth while studying the well-established, international principles which will determine whether the desired changes will be successful and achieve the intended result. Failure to adhere to these principles will inevitably lead to disaster.

General principles
of organisational change

What do we mean by organisational change? At its heart we mean a change in the way people within the organisation actually behave on a day-to-day basis: the way they interact with each other and the way they interact with the world outside their organisation. Changing the structure or processes within an organisation may be part of the necessary change, but these things are secondary. The key is to change everybody's normal day-to-day attitudes and behaviour to achieve a desired outcome or set of outcomes from the organisation as a whole. In essence we are trying to change their way of thinking and acting collectively.

Any effective change must come from within the organisation: it cannot be imposed from the outside, or there will be a strong tendency to reject it. An effective change is only possible if all employees buy in personally to the need for the change, so that they are fully committed to it. If they do not, the change will not be sustained.

Change must be for a clearly defined purpose, i.e.:

- be undertaken for a good reason
- have a clear direction and if possible a visionary end point
- be capable of eliciting an emotional attachment in the members of the organisation

This creates a *pull* in the direction of the desired change. In addition the leadership of the organisation must be fully committed to the change themselves, which means that:

- they must articulate it clearly, underlining the reasons why it is necessary, and the desired end point (outcome)
- they must do this for an extended period of time (perhaps for as much as two to three years) to maintain clarity and avoid confusion in the minds of their departments' employees – there must be constancy of purpose
- they must personally live the change at all times, meaning that everything they do must be consistent with the desired end point
- they must recognise that their behaviour is highly visible to their subordinates, and any off-message behaviour on their part will be seized on as evidence that they do not themselves really believe the message that they are espousing – i.e. that they are not serious about the change initiative

Particularly if the change is urgent, it helps greatly if the current situation is recognised by all to be untenable (i.e. 'it would be uncomfortable/impossible for all to continue as we are').

This creates an impetus to move away from the status quo (*push*) – but it is essentially directionless, which is why it must be combined with the above-mentioned visionary end point to provide an attractive direction in which to move.

It is not necessary, nor indeed is it desirable, for the MoD military and civilian leadership to spell out in detail *how* the change should take place (i.e. what specifically should each individual do differently).

They must, however spell out *where* MoD needs to move to, and *why*.

For the change to be accepted and internalised by the organisation, all those working within MoD must be involved in working out the how together. Members of MoD, be they soldiers or civil servants, are in the best position to know what needs to change in their own work environment to create the desired change and they need to be given the freedom to decide upon and implement those changes themselves. This will create a situation in which the change is regarded as their own, and they will therefore be committed to it.

Problems with traditional change processes

Change is usually attempted by trying to spread it throughout the organisation via a relatively small number of change agents (internal or occasionally external), whose job it is to lead improvement initiatives and to train groups of people to do likewise.

Because the number of change agents is small, and the number of people they can train is also small, these people represent only a tiny proportion of the whole organisation. Their ideas tend to be rejected by the rest of the organisation who have not been involved in their development. Demotivation ensues, some change agents/trainees will give up, and the process has to be repeated over and over again in order to gain traction for the change.

Over time, somewhat grudgingly, the organisation will change, but the process will be slow, stressful to participants, and very wasteful of time and resources for the organisation.

For large organisations like MoD, the problem is much worse. Effective change using the above approach can take years, if it happens at all, as the few change agents have to fight the inertia or active obstruction of thousands. On top of this, the leadership of the organisation may well be tempted eventually to change course, which of course torpedoes the initiative in the eyes of everyone, and serves to make them think that they were right to oppose it in the first place.

Even if the MoD leadership sticks to its guns, there will be a tendency for them to impose a plethora of reinforcement actions, often of a strongly coercive nature, and this will simply build resentment.

Overall, this kind of change process is costly in terms of resources and time, and low on effectiveness. It is possible to speed up this process somewhat by employing a larger number of change agents, but cost will be much higher, and consistency of the change message is likely to suffer as it is being channelled through a larger number of individuals.

The solution

The way to avoid these problems is to approach the whole process in a radically different manner. It is best to change the whole organisation at the same time (or at least within a very short time scale). This means involving everybody in MoD in the change process, and ensuring that they are all moving in the same direction simultaneously. Even if we achieve only a small change initially we have created movement across the whole organisation, and we can repeat the process to build and sustain the momentum of change in the desired direction. Because everybody is involved, there is little or no resistance from the unchanged organisation (no part of the organisation is unchanged). Everybody is at the same stage in the process at the same time, so peer pressure in this case operates to reinforce the change process rather than working against it.

For this approach to work in MoD, the process must be (or at least appear to be) internally driven. It should be collective (team-based) rather than a series of individual initiatives (to build peer pressure and collective will). Ideally it should be implemented through the internal hierarchy of the organisation itself (to tie all levels of the organisation together in the collective enterprise).

The essential steps in the process are described below, but the focus is on getting everyone in the organisation to work together in groups of six to eight people to develop tangible ideas for improvement (consistent with the desired change), which they themselves implement, thus creating the initial movement of the organisation in the desired direction. The ideas come from within (at work group level) and are implemented locally (also at work group level). Because everyone in the organisation is involved (including the leadership and all intermediate levels) the ideas generated will be very wide ranging and once implemented will collectively result in a step change in the organisation's performance.

A key point will be the role and attitude of the MoD leadership towards these multiple proposed changes. Traditionally they would wish to vet, i.e. control, the changes that people make, but their focus should instead be on support, i.e. removing obstacles that inhibit the changes. In this way people feel empowered and that they are a vital part of the process, which results in strong buy-in throughout the whole organisation.

This apparent lack of control may make the MoD leadership nervous because they are no longer controlling every aspect of what people do. They need to move from micro-managing/controlling to being supportive, and from focusing on defined processes (just following the rules and all the steps in the process) to being outcome-focused (doing whatever it takes to get the desired outcome).

It should be stressed that the process through which the ideas are generated is not a free-for-all. Whilst it deliberately does not control the specific solutions that people generate, it must and does control the sequence and orientation of the discussions that lead to those solutions. The process is of course designed to elicit solutions that are consistent with the desired overall change.

This type of change process is particularly suitable for organisations like MoD with large numbers of staff, and is not only relatively quick but also highly cost-effective. It utilises the organisation's own people to drive and sustain the change and results are apparent very quickly (within days or months, rather than years).

Key steps in the approach

1. Define drivers of change and direction of change

- What is the current state of the organisation? A clear understanding of the organisation's current culture, structure and key processes needs to be built in some depth. This will require research and interviewing of people at different levels in the organisation.

- The purpose of the organisation and who it exists for (i.e. who are its customers, suppliers or any other stakeholders?) must be clearly understood and articulated.

- Why change is needed, and who is saying so, must be clearly understood; e.g. cost effectiveness, poor service quality, slow decision making.

- What future state would the organisation ideally have, i.e. what would be seen as the normal/routine behaviour of the organisation once that state has been reached?

- Why is that state wanted? Who would benefit from it?

The above defines the starting point and the desired direction of change, and the reasons why we need to make the change. This information provides the framework for the design of the change process, along with a great deal of context that will inform the design as well.

2. Sequence for effective learning and change

Provide Context, to include:

- What's the problem/why change?
  - including consequences of not changing (make personal)

- Information
  - specific data to illustrate issues
  - can be auto-generated i.e. based on participants' own experiences. This is usually best because it is more tangible/real to participants.
  - or use example survey data from outside the organisation
  - or a combination of both (in which case start with the external data and make it real by illustrating from participants' own experience)

- Take everyone through a discussion process (in groups of six to eight people) which:
  - uses a learning rather than instructional approach (self-discovery has more meaning and value to people and builds buy-in)
  - is based around problems/issues known to/regularly experienced by participants, because these have most relevance to their daily work life

- Take context and information, discuss and build collective understanding to get:
  - intellectual buy-in to problem – 'I understand it'
  - emotional buy-in – 'I (personally) want to do something about it'
  - follow a (provided) universal process to collectively develop a solution to a specific problem
  - at the same time learn that the universal process is applicable to any problem/issue
  - achieve an outcome (solution)

- Outcome
  - a recognisably good solution to a known problem
  - it's our solution – we developed it, we own it and buy in to it

- the process works!
- maybe this is not so difficult after all!
- move to action: develop an action plan which is : specific, measurable, achievable, relevant, time-bound
- focus on 'my personal action', not that of others (though the process will collect and potentially redistribute actions for others)
- identify the support I need to enable me to act
- who will do what, by when? (focus on immediate future, to get quick wins)
- what will I measure (to ensure I've succeeded)?
- what will the customer see? (measured in terms of what is important to them)
- what's in it for me?

- more things to do in short term perhaps, but balanced against elimination of useless work and frustration

- self-worth – what I'm doing is important/useful/necessary so I feel good

- this part must be both intellectual and emotional to be effective

The outcomes from the process are generally as follows (for everyone in the organisation):

- a good understanding of what we are trying to do and why

- personal identification with this (I want to be part of it)

- starting the process by dealing with one or more day–to-day issues and finding a solution, which I am immediately implementing.

- realisation that I have now learned a process which I can apply to any such issues (and I have many). I'm off to a running start, and so is everyone else in the organisation.

The above discussion sequence is embedded in a tool called a Learning Tool, which ensures that the flow and logic of the discussion is always consistent across the many hundreds or thousands of groups taking part.

3. Support and reinforcement

- This is necessary to ensure this is not just a one-off or short term sequence of events but is seen as part of a continuous process of change in a specified direction.
  - Multiple reinforcement actions over time will be necessary
  - Provided by the management structure within the organisation (i.e. not coming from outside)
  - Carefully designed in advance - will require training of management to ensure effectiveness

Applicability

The above generic change process can be applied to achieve a multiplicity of aims (not all at the same time). Some examples:

- values/ethos of the organisation and translation into appropriate related departmental and individual behaviours
- customer focus – building it/embedding it/ strengthening it
- process improvement with the customer of the process as the primary focus (i.e. outcome-

focused) – contrary to received wisdom the outcome is changing over time and therefore the process must continually evolve. Process orientation does not mean ossification of the organisation.

- Innovation: in a rapidly changing world any organisation must continually examine whether what it is doing remains relevant to its customers. It must reinvent itself if not.

- empowerment of staff members, moving an organisation from top-down rigid control to employees empowered to do whatever it takes to achieve an outcome (within agreed broad constraints)

The process is then tailored to deliver the specific desired change.

Conclusion

The above approach has form and has been proved to deliver quick results in large organisations. Like any major initiative, it takes determination on the part of senior management and it also requires constancy of focus on their part for a period of time that is measured in years rather than days. Also essential, of course, is that political leaders need to be (and remain) clear about what practical capabilities and capacity MoD is trying to build for the future.

The UK Defence Industry: Time to Reconsider?

David McOwat

Introduction

This brief personal interpretation of the defence industry is designed to provoke a reconsideration of UK research, industrial, and defence industrial strategies. I suggest that the reduction of the conventional UK defence budget to some 1.5 per cent (the two per cent GDP figure includes the nuclear deterrent) cannot support past strategies. The new investment level demands a new strategic conceptual framework and operational concepts[1], based on agility and the capacity to generate a range of powers appropriate to the demands of the campaigns. This is a complex, not complicated, problem where changes in parts affect the evolution of the whole, and in unexpected ways.

Since UK industry excels in the small and medium-sized enterprise (SME) sector, and this sector provides the agility we seek, I suggest that we should base the industrial strategy in this sector, supported by resuscitated defence and industrial research capacity. This is no panacea, but may stimulate a reconsideration of our competitive stance and the strategies that accompany it.

The defence 'market'

The term *defence market* is a misnomer. There is no market mechanism involved, in the textbook sense. Defence is a political issue, regarded as the primary responsibility of governments. The defence 'market' changes to reflect the size of defence forces needed to address the levels of global and regional instabilities, but also to reflect the use of the suppliers of defence equipment and services as a form of power in themselves.

As the current global hegemon, it is not surprising that the US defence budget is now some 50 per cent of the global total and their defence industry correspondingly dominates. The US defence suppliers have been organised into an oligopoly of prime contractors by US governments, partly to exercise industrial power. The research needed to sustain this dominance is primarily funded by the US government, through DoD, DOE and other departments and agencies, and includes an extensive open source technical intelligence programme. However, it is also able to draw on the largest advanced engineering economy in the world and defence industrial policies that subsidise the defence suppliers.

Other developed countries have followed this strategy of government-sponsored oligopoly but have had less success in providing equivalent research and industrial policy. China and Russia have begun to challenge the US dominance, but are still well behind overall. Both have very large technical intelligence programmes, with the Chinese being particularly successful in exploiting western academic research.

The UK and France attempted to compete with the USA during the Cold War but have lost their competitive stance with the reductions in investment volume and a willingness to transfer responsibility for their defence to the NATO Alliance – i.e. the USA. They were successful while the (conventional) defence budget exceeded some four per cent GDP, industrial manufacturing was globally competitive, and defence research comprised ten per cent of the equipment budget supported by a significant industrial R&D budget.

Prime contractors emerged in response to the growing technical complexity in major defence systems brought about by measure-countermeasure competition, and the very long lifetimes of the systems. A single vertically integrated company could not support the range of technical expertise required over the period, but needed the expertise of a network of companies which could co-operate to produce and sustain the system.

Sustaining design, research and development teams between projects has become unaffordable for commercial companies and requires government support. The financial and managerial challenges this created were originally overseen by governments, but these too have been transferred to the primes, and have become the primary function of the primes. In turn, this has increased the difficulty in contracting effectively as governments have reduced the technical and managerial competence of their defence departments in their search for greater efficiency.

The small and medium-sized enterprises (SMEs) continue to provide a vital contribution to the defence sector, both as contributors to the primes' supply-chain networks and as suppliers themselves. They dominate small-production-run advanced equipment and services used in campaigns where agility and adaptability are pre-eminent, e.g. counter-insurgency, counter-terrorism and information warfare. The intellectual base for much of this has come from academic, industrial and commercial research. The success of this sector is reflected in its lack of publicity! Recent campaigns have drawn heavily on this sector, rather than equipment and services provided by the primes, and use a completely different agile acquisition system, similar to that advocated elsewhere in this paper.

The current UK situation

In recent years UK governments have reduced the defence budget, but with no compensating reduction in the scope of equipment and services they require, only a reduction in quantity. The conventional defence budget is now closer to 1.5 per cent of GDP than two. They have persisted in a policy of a government-sponsored oligopoly of prime contractors ('primes') – the political-industrial complex – delivering the equipment and the services, in an attempt to pass risk from political to industrial responsibility and 'simplify' acquisition. They have compensated for some of the reduction in volume by contractorising equipment support and services to the existing and a few new primes. BAE Systems remains the dominant prime, but it is now more American than British. Indeed, most of the primes are now foreign-owned. The inclusion of through-life support has had the effect of reducing the equipment acquisition and research budgets, making the equipment primes less able to provide next generation systems. However, there are no requirements visible for major new systems that would keep the primes busy and encourage investment. The current budget cannot fund the existing generation.

The defence R&D volume collapsed with the privatisation of the bulk of MOD research to Qinetiq. Qinetiq has been forced to become an equipment supplier in order to generate commercial rates of return and compete with the other UK and US defence suppliers, rather than function as a privatised research supplier to UK defence companies. Similarly, the DTI R&D budget has collapsed, perhaps to pay for UK contributions to the EC Research Programmes (Framework and its successors). However, the EC programmes are of little use to the defence sector. The loss of technical competence in MOD, civil and military, has reduced the capacity of MOD to function as an intelligent and expert customer.

UK industry cannot sustain the investment needed for the long-term research (beyond five years to use) typical of leading-edge capabilities, where it may take forty years to deploy the knowledge in systems. UK academic research meets some of the need but no longer pursues the range of engineering research required for defence and, where it does, the research students are often not UK nationals. BAE Systems has closed its corporate research laboratories.

With the collapse in the defence budget, and defence and industrial R&D, the UK primes amalgamated and attacked the US and Middle East markets with government assistance. In the 2013 financial year, US subsidiaries made BAE Systems the eighth largest DoD contractor, accounting for some eight per cent of the DoD budget. It remains a major supplier to Saudi Arabia. The increase in BAE Systems' DoD volume has been accompanied by an increase in US contractors' share of the UK defence market.

The UK economy has seen the manufacturing proportion fall dramatically as the government emphasised financial services. This has reduced the base available for the defence sector to draw on and increased their costs, as they now have to bear the total costs. If the UK is to sustain a defence industry, it requires an advanced industrial civil sector as a foundation for a revived form of dual-use-military adaptation of civil systems.

The European Commission

The European Commission (EC) remains dominated by those whose strategy is to create a United States of Europe, with an advanced civil industry able to compete with the USA as a peer and an integrated military supplied by a European defence industry.[2] It has had great success in its civil industrial objectives, including a civil R&D programme sufficient to support the industries.

However, the EC has been unable to convince all the member states either to cede the control of defence, or to increase their defence budgets to US levels, and there is no equivalent defence R&D programme. The European defence industry has responded by mergers to create European primes based on civil/military corporations. EADS was an example of this policy, as was their proposal to merge with BAE Systems in summer 2012 to create a European competitor to the US defence corporations. However, the purpose of the merger appears to have had more to do with EADS acquiring a large stake in the US (and UK) markets than any prospect of creating a viable European defence prime supplying the European defence market. It is unclear whether the US Congress would have allowed the merger to proceed, given their competitive stance.

Political and strategic considerations

The long lifecycle of major defence systems means that they cannot be owned solely by one government but should be supervised by parliament as a whole, for the investment required to achieve value from them will require action by successive governments of perhaps different persuasions.

Parliament must therefore have mechanisms to form and review defence capacity, its volume, balance and health.

Similarly, the long-term research required needs parliamentary oversight. Parliament must therefore 'own' defence strategy. This requires many more members to be informed on statecraft, defence and technical matters. Parliament should provide education and training courses for those interested who lack the background.

Perhaps the most challenging issue concerns finance, for defence is not an annual expenditure, but a strategic long-term investment. Funding it annually is inappropriate. Other means need to be developed, as argued elsewhere in this volume, to provide MoD with access to long-term investment funds, and to encourage industry to support their development of invention and innovation capacity.

Finally, if we are to retain a national defence industrial capacity, parliament has to reconsider the UK's competitive stance and create the political/industrial complex able to achieve this. The problem is not industry's alone.

Alternative courses of action

With this as our starting point, we need to consider how the political/industrial complex needs to evolve to meet UK needs if we want to rebuild our competitive stance. Such a change implies a different defence industrial strategy that will confer asymmetric advantage to the UK. I suggest that this requires:

- Reform of the political components of the political/industrial complex to change ownership of defence and research strategy to parliament rather than government. We must educate the politicians interested in security and re-skill the departments, especially MoD, changing the attitudes and behaviour of its staff, raising aspirations, and reintroducing technical competencies. This requires new leadership that will operate in collaboration with and in support of existing personnel, many of whom already possess the necessary skills and knowledge, and to empower them to set aside existing procedures and processes. The challenge will be for ministers and officials to provide and enable this leadership rather than writing off the problem as being just too difficult.

- Development of an appropriate funding system to support the log-term investment required by defence whilst retaining parliamentary oversight

- Building our acquisition capability and capacity on the basis of our whole industry and economy, not just on a separate defence industry. This does not just refer to pieces of equipment. The future capabilities and capacities we will need are just as likely to be services with people as their main component – think *intelligence* or *cyber*. We do not want to preserve or rebuild the old forces we had; we want to build new, relevant forces which will be radically different.

- Adopting a defence industrial strategy based on supporting the network of existing SMEs and those that would emerge from dismantling some of the primes. The dismantling process would need government facilitation and advice from the financial sector. Encouraging management buy-outs would keep the local organisations and empower them to get rid of the top layer of redundant management. These companies will need to do both civilian and military work if they are to succeed. As we have noted elsewhere in this study, the UK's Formula One provides a most successful example of this kind of network system. The strength of the new network of smaller companies would depend upon an effective network for the industry, perhaps created from the existing trade association. MoD would need to provide strategic leadership to the research side in co-operation with academia, industry and commerce. With the reduced scale of our forces, increased emphasis needs to be placed on design, and the (highly successful) model of a Soviet Design Bureau or the US Skunk Works, combining design, R&D and prototype production, and generating competition between designers rather than between producers (as production runs will be so small).

- Rebuilding the UK advanced manufacturing sector, stimulated by research investment

- Rebuilding the defence research programme. Without this, we will not be able to produce anything special which will give us an edge, or which others will want to buy. We need to harness academic, civilian and defence research, and to understand how to acquire and exploit world knowledge.

- Reconsidering academic policy to support UK students in departments that are able to support MoD needs, or establishing if this can be achieved by dramatically expanding the Defence Academy to create the equivalent of a major technical university.

- Recognising the need for industry/academe/ government collaboration in order to develop rapidly new capabilities in support of experimental formations at an advanced capability development centre, based on a merger of the Centre for Defence Enterprise with Dstl and the Defence Academy. This would also house a dramatically enlarged technical intelligence capability.

Notes

Overiew

1   Christopher Elliott Hurst, *High Command, British Military Leadership in the Iraq and Afghanistan Wars*, London 2015

2   Haus Curiosities, *Britain in a Perilous World, the Strategic Defence and Security Review We Need*, Jonathan Shaw, London 2014

3   Peter Hennessy, Haus Curiosities, *Establishment and Meritocracy*, London, 2014

4   Global Trends 2030, Alternative Worlds, A Publication of the National Intelligence Council, Washington, 2012

5   The Original order was intended to be 138 JSFs for RAF &RN. In July 2012, Defence Secretary Hammond stated that an initial 48 F-35Bs would be purchased to equip the single carrier then planned to be brought into service, but a final figure of F-35 purchases would not be decided until the Strategic Defence and Security Review in 2015. To equip 2 carriers will require a further 48 aircraft. It was also suggested that the UK may later purchase F-35A variants to replace the countrys Eurofighter Typhoon fleet. To date, the UK has actually bought 4 combat capable aircraft to add to our 4 test aircraft. Gareth Jennings, London - IHS Janes Defence Weekly. 23 November 2014

6   In the House of Commons Standard Note SN/SG/03139 20120705 *The Cost Of International Military Operations*, it is estimated that 'the net additional cost of international military operations in Iraq, Afghanistan and Libya between 2001/02 and 2012/13 is estimated to be almost £30bn.' The equipment involved was mainly acquired through the Urgent Operational Requirements (UOR) process, involving many thousands of UORs. Security considerations prevent a detailed analysis.

7   See for example Science, Engineering & Technology (SET) Statistics published by ONS on behalf of BIS. This describes Research in terms of the Frascati definitions. It clearly shows the reduction in Applied Strategic Research from £196m 2001-02 to £3m in 2012-13., in constant 2012 prices; Specific Research appears to have been protected since it has a broadly flat profile over this period; while Experimental Development has roughly halved from £2Bn to £0.9Bn This must inject risk into MoDs acquisitions.

8   See: *Reach for the Skies – A Strategic Vision for UK Aerospace* – The Aerospace Growth Partnership – Industry and Government working together to secure the future for UK aerospace, BIS on gov.uk

9   We can find no appropriate studies in the open literature on the volume of Defence Budget required. We hope that this is not the case within Government. The NATO 2 per cent GDP figure was an unsuccessful attempt to increase the proportion of the NATO budget contributed by affluent European members, most of whom exploited the USA contribution to avoid defence expenditure in favour of their own affluence. It was not based on any analysis of the contributions needed, nor did it attempt to determine whether it would provide value for money. Now that the UK is likely to further reduce its Defence Budget to below 2 per cent of GDP, there is a greater likelihood that NATO itself may collapse. Russia appears to be exploiting the weakened political resolve within NATO in its attacks on Ukraine.

10   In the UKTI DSO Defence & Security Export Figures for 2013, UK ranks 11th in defence exports, and 8th in imports. UK export orders of defence equipment and services were estimated to have reached their highest level in 2013 since the series began in 1988, at just under £9.8 billion. This increase can be attributed to new orders for Agusta-Westland helicopters from Norway and South Korea, in addition to strong on-going business across the Middle East region.

11   See 'How MoD Works' V4.1 Sep 2014, on gov.co.uk

12   MoD DASA DERP Inter-generational equipment cost escalation – N Davies, A Eager, M Maier, L Penfold 20121218 suggest that there is some evidence of a reduction in overall defence inflation, but that further evidence is required.

13   We have forgotten that: 'Quantity has a quality all of its own'. LENIN, quoted in J. F. Dunnigans *How to Make War*

14   'I can tell the House today that, after two years work, the black hole in the defence budget has finally been eliminated and the budget is now in balance, with a small annual reserve built in as a prudent measure to make sure that we are not blown off course by unforeseen events: a plan endorsed by the chiefs and by the Treasury.

     Under the previous Government, the equipment plan became meaningless because projects were committed to it without the funding to pay for them, creating a fantasy programme. Systematic over-programming was compounded by a 'conspiracy of optimism', with officials, the armed forces and suppliers consistently planning on a best-case scenario, in the full knowledge that once a project had been committed to, they could revise up costs with little consequence. It was an overheated equipment plan, managed on a hand-to-mouth basis and driven by short-term cash, rather than long-term value. There were constant postponements and renegotiations, driving costs into projects in a self-reinforcing spiral of busted budgets and torn-up timetables. Rigid contracting meant that there was no flexibility to respond to changed threat priorities or to alternative technologies becoming available. It is our armed forces and the defence of our country that have ultimately paid the price for that mismanagement. The culture and the practice have to change. We will move forward with a new financial discipline in the equipment plan. There will be under-programming rather than over-programming, so that we can focus on value rather than on cash management. That will give our armed forces confidence that once a project is in the programme, it is real, funded and will be delivered, so that they can plan with certainty. The core committed equipment programme, which covers investment in new equipment and data systems, and their support, amounts to just under £152 billion over 10 years, against a total planned spend of almost £160 billion. That £152 billion includes, for the first time ever, an effective centrally held contingency reserve, determined by Bernard Gray, the new Chief of Defence Matériel, of more than £4 billion to ensure the robustness of the plan'.

The Secretary of State for Defence (Rt Hon Philip Hammond), Hansard 14 May 2012 : Column 261

15 Defence departmental resources: 2013, 26 September 2013 Table 1.03.04 suggests that Frascati R&D has dropped from £2.1B to 1.3Bn of a total 'R&D' that has dropped from 2.7 to £2Bn. The Science, Engineering and Technology analyses published by ONS and BIS annually two years in arrears, suggest an alarming reduction in Applied Strategic Research from £196M 2001-02 to £3M in 2012-13., in constant 2012 prices; Specific Research appears to have been protected since it has a broadly flat profile over this period; while Experimental Development has roughly halved from £2Bn to £0.9Bn. This injects risk into our Programme, and denies future advanced capabilities.

16 Other than when rapidly acquiring systems.

17 For example, merging the Defence Academy with Dstl would assist this.

18 The 1985 Defence Review created the Commitments organization to discharge a similar function. It is unclear to the outsider how much of this has survived the contraction of MoD.

19 Including the EU Research Programme, which is the World's largest.

20 For an excellent explanation of the importance of having a national presence in a key area of the world to advance our national interest, see the article by Lt Gen Sir Simon Mayall in the current (June 2014) edition of the official British Army Yearbook.

Chapter 1

1 The Treasury allow MoD a one per cent inflation rate on major equipment. See also Footnote 2 below.

2 *Declinism* is an attitude of mind which assumes that the country is in permanent, irreversible decline, causing the individual or institution to adopt a consequent pattern of behaviour which actually brings the decline about. To confuse the legitimate need of government to reduce defence spending and to reform the military establishment in response to the changing security environment with the shrinking of the country's might due to national decline demonstrates a failure of strategic thinking.

Chapter 2

1 MoD, *How Defence Works*, V4.1 2014. pp34,35, URL: https://www.gov.uk/government/publications/how-defence-works-the-defence-operating-model

2 The 1985 Defence Review created the Commitments organisation to discharge a similar function. It is unclear to the outsider how much of this has survived the contraction of MoD.

3 Public Broadcasting Service, 'The Blair Doctrine: Full transcript', speech delivered to the Economic Club, Chicago, 22 April 1999, URL: http://www.pbs.org/newshour/bb/international-jan-june99-blair_doctrine4-23/

4 The Centre for Defence Economics at the University of York, founded by Prof Keith Hartley, is the leading UK centre for the topic. There are many relevant publications, including a 2010 PhD thesis by Peter MacDonald on the "Economics of Military Outsourcing".

5 The major UK studies on defence inflation are to be found in numerous papers and books by Prof D L Kirkpatrick, and the late P G Pugh. MoD has paid insufficient attention to this body of work in recent years, and appears to have lost sight of the origins in measure-countermeasure competitive performance. With no budgetary increase, a defence inflator of eight per cent pa on a 25-year replacement cycle will reduce a fleet size to only some 16 per cent of the original after 25 years. This rises to 31 per cent with an inflator five per cent and 62 per cent with an inflator of two per cent. Increasing the cycle time delays but does not solve the effect. Pugh, Kirkpatrick and in the USA, Norman Augustine, suggest that the defence inflator is up eight per cent p.a. in the case of fighter aircraft and other similar complex weapon systems, and even in the case of B-vehicles is at least one per cent. Overall the equipment budget inflates at about 6 per cent, it appears. A recent paper by MoD (DERP 20121218 Inter-generational equipment cost escalation - N Davies, *et al*) questions

these figures, but unconvincingly and inconclusively. The general reduction in fleet sizes across the industrialized economies suggests that it is a genuine phenomenon, and that UK acquisition is not alone today in facing the necessity of invention in equipment and operational concepts. Small fleets rapidly reach a point of negative value, i.e. where they cannot afford to lose any of their number, even in training. In war, a weapon you cannot afford to lose is a weapon you cannot afford to use.

6   From 2014, R&D expenditure will contribute to the compilation of the value of the UK's net worth and be included as part of Gross Domestic Product (GDP) estimates.

7   See for example Science, Engineering & Technology (SET) Statistics published by ONS on behalf of BIS. This describes Research in terms of the Frascati definitions. It clearly shows the reduction in Applied Strategic Research from £196M 2001-02 to £3M in 2012-13., in constant 2012 prices; Specific Research appears to have been protected since it has a broadly flat profile over this period; while Experimental Development has roughly halved from £2Bn to £0.9Bn This must inject risk into MoD's acquisitions.

8   DASA Statistics put the MoD Intramural Research at £106m, most of which is in Dstl.

9   For example: In 1995 BAE took the decision to get out of aircraft manufacturing as there was not enough profit margin. The corporate research facility at Bristol finally closed in 2000. Their merger with MDS closed their research labs, as they had earlier closed Ferranti's labs. BAE no longer has the capability to design advanced military aircraft - no adequate facilities, designers, physical engineering infrastructure. The design of all current aircraft currently being produced in the UK is based on research from before 2000, even for UAVs. MoD & BIS are currently trying to regenerate a UK capability via a range of initially small initiatives, which hopefully will over time address these issues. Meanwhile we face a large capability gap.

10 Dr Ronald Kostoff, formerly Director of Basic Research, ONR, in numerous papers.

11 Ministry of Defence, Annual Statistical Series 1, Finance Bulletin 1.03, Departmental Resources 2013, 26 September 2013, Table 1.03.05, p.12   https://www.gov.uk/government/uploads/ system/uploads/attachment_data/file/397351/Annual_statistical _series_1_finance_bulletin_1_03_departmental_reources_2013.pdf

12 Life-Cycle: The life-cycle includes a long period before a system exists and extends to include its disposal and any associated remediation. This is partly associated with the timescales needed

for the invention of new systems, and partly with the time to realise needed systems. New science typically takes some 40 years to see application, engineering some 15 years to mature, and manufacture around 5 years. Systems based on new services may see immediate use directly from research; equipment-based systems take much longer to realise, depending on the novel content. Synthesis of extant knowledge allows systems to be realised and acquired in a matter of months; invention takes many years.

13　Formal stages of the evaluation process: MoD, through its observation of global trends, should forecast the potential or actual need for new *Equipment Concepts*, and identify inadequacies in the current inventory, within its evolving set of *Operational Concepts* that collectively implement its *Strategic Conceptual Framework*.

The systems, once acquired, become part of the overall inventory that suitably educated and selected *personnel* employ to generate the forms of power needed to advance UK Interests in the a range of *Campaigns*. The inventory is managed as a whole to ensure the availability of the systems and their continuing relevance to the current *Estimate* of future capability.

The *Estimate Process* determines whether to modify systems, either to exploit new technical opportunities that increase the value of the system, or to meet the evolving needs of Campaigns, or to dispose of the systems. Disposal may incur significant costs, generate income or contribute to advancing UK interests. Systems consumed in campaigns may need to be replaced, where the Estimate requires this, or replaced by new concepts.

Campaign Planning identifies both the systems needed to undertake the campaign successfully in the *Campaign Systems Plan*, but also accelerates the Estimate and Conceptual assessment of the *value* of the *Inventory*.

14　The move of the Procurement Executive from London to Bristol resulted in its losing 40 per cent of its technically literate staff. A further reform, as recently proposed, will likely remove the rest.

15　Individual Foreign Shareholding Restrictions: The Articles of Association include a requirement that no foreign person, or foreign persons acting in concert, can have more than a 15 per cent voting interest in the Company. This current provision in the Articles can only be amended with the consent of the holder of the Special Share, the Secretary of State for Business, Innovation and Skills. The foreign shareholding restriction in the Company has changed over time as shown below, having been last amended in 2002 to reflect the above position.

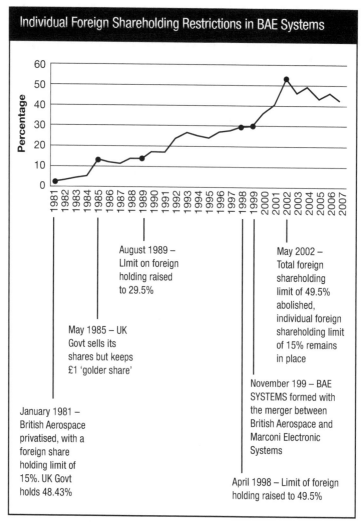

Source: BAE

16 They will not be limited to armed forces: we must generate a wide range of forms of power, all of which will require products and services to be acquired.

The Strategic Environment

1 House of Commons Debate, 1 March 1848, Hansard vol 97 cc122

The Evolving Asymmetric Threat and the Irrelevance of Structures

1   MoD, 'Strategic Trends Programme: Future Character of Conflict', 2 February 2010, URL: https://www.gov.uk/government/publications/future-character-of-conflict

2   Guidelines for achieving a 24-month gap between six-month long deployments so as to reduce the strain on personnel and families to an acceptable level.

Acquisition and the Special Relationship

1   Dwight D. Eisenhower, State of the Union address to a joint session of Congress, 9 January 1958

The Operationalisation of Defence Industries: The Critical Military Component

1   Sun Tzu, *The Art of War* (tr. Samuel B. Griffith) (Oxford: Oxford University Press, 1963)

2   Trevor Taylor, 'The limited capacity of management to rescue UK defence policy: a review and a word of caution', *International Affairs* 88:2 (London: Royal Institute of International Affairs, 2012).

3   Paul Cornish and Andrew Dorman, 'National Defence in the Age of Austerity', *International Affairs* 85:4 (London: Royal Institute of International Affairs, 2012).

4   Jacques Derrida's seminal theoretical work includes *Of Grammatology* (1967) and *The Politics of Friendship* (1994).

5   See Hugh McManners, *Gulf War One: The Truth from Those Who Were There* (London: Random House, 2010).

6   See McManners, *Gulf War One*.

7   See Henrik Heidenkamp, 'Sustaining the UK's Defence Effort: Contractor Support to Operations Market Dynamics' (London: RUSI, 2012).

8   See Jacques S. Gansler, *Democracy's Arsenal: Creating a Twenty-First Century Defense Industry* (Boston: Massachusetts Institute of Technology, 2011).

9   See Henrik Heidenkamp, John Louth and Trevor Taylor, 'The Defence Industrial Ecosystem: Delivering Security in an Uncertain World' (London: RUSI, 2011)

10   As reported in *The Times* (London) on 3 May 2011.See also IISS, The Military Balance 2011 (London: Routledge, 2011).

11   See: www.publications.parliament.uk/pa/cm201011cmselect/cmtreasury/544 (as of 31.05.2011).

12 See Heidenkamp *et. al.* The Defence Industrial Ecosystem.

13 By 'engineer' I refer to professional chartered engineers, skilled tradesmen/women, including electrical and installation engineers and technicians, and those personnel in training.

14 Oxford Economics (2011) 'The Economic Contribution of BAE Systems to the UK in 2009', Oxford: Abbey House.

15 All at 2009 prices.

16 BAE Systems productivity was £78,175 whilst the economic average was £42,200. The UK estimated average for the manufacturing sector was £58,300.

17 Jobs dependent on the company either directly or through supply chains stimulate consumer spending in the wider economy. These can be described as the induced benefits to the UK economy.

18 The author is grateful to the management of the Barrow shipyard for allowing interviews to be undertaken in 2012 to inform this work.

The Evolution of Governance of National Security

1 It is very difficult to get exact numbers for the size of the Cabinet Office and No. 10, to include all attachments and outlying offices.

2 The Conservative Party, 'A Resilient Nation: National Security Green Paper', Policy Green Paper No.13, 2009, URL: https://www.conservatives.com/~/media/Files/Green%20Papers/National_Security_Green_Paper.ashx?dl=true

3 The Police Service has also been seriously affected, but this is outside the scope of the current paper.

4 Nor is this an issue only in the MoD. The Police Service has been similarly affected by this culture and is now led by a generation of senior officers who have been promoted for avoiding risk. The Commissioner of the Metropolitan Police Service recently described his job as 'being primarily a risk manager'.

Whitehall's Strategic Deficit

1 Orwell, G., 'Politics and the English Language', from an online version of the essay, available at wikilivres.ca, URL: http://wikilivres.ca/wiki/Politics_and_the_English_Language (accessed 20 April 2015)

2 Hurd, RT Hon Lord D., *The Search For Peace*, Little, Brown, 1997, pp.250-51

The F.I.R.E. Approach to Defence Acquisitions

1 Lt. Col. Dan Ward served as an acquisitions officer in the U.S. Air Force for over 20 years. The views expressed in this article are solely those of the author and do not reflect the official policy or position of the U.S. Air Force.

2   Ward, D., *F.I.R.E.: How Fast, Inexpensive, Restrained and Elegant Methods Ignite Innovation*, HarperBusiness, 2014.

3   Standish Group, 'Chaos Manifesto 2013: Think big, act small', 2013, URL: http://www.versionone.com/assets/img/files/ChaosManifesto2013.pdf

4   Taleb, Nassim, *Antifragile: Things that Gain from Disorder*, Penguin, 2013.

5   McCurdy, Howard, *Faster, Better, Cheaper: Low-Cost Innovation in the US Space Program*, Johns Hopkins University Press, 2001, p.59

A New Acquisition Process to Acquire What We Need From What We Have Got Available

1   OGC, 'Best Practice Portfolio', 2011, URL: http://webarchive.nationalarchives.gov.uk/20100503135839/http://www.ogc.gov.uk/documents/OGC_Best_Practice_Portfolio.pdf

2   See the gov.uk website, 'National Infrastructure Plan', URL: https://www.gov.uk/government/collections/national-infrastructure-plan

The UK Defence Industry: Time to Reconsider?s

1   The issue of changing the strategic conceptual framework and operational concepts is considered elsewhere.

2   The EU's Future of Europe group of 11 foreign ministers – led by German MFA Westerwelle and including the French and Spanish foreign ministers but not including William Hague – which met on 17 September 2012, when BAE Systems/EADS merger negotiations were underway, concluded that Europe needed a more active foreign policy and an integrated European army, backed up by a stronger European defence industry.